THE AFRICAN ELEPHANT
LAST DAYS OF EDEN

Boyd Norton

Foreword by Richard E. Leakey
Introduction by the African Wildlife Foundation

VOYAGEUR PRESS

*To John Lidede of Kenya and Hussein Hamisi of Tanzania, two of Africa's finest safari guides and drivers.
Each is* rafiki na ndugu, *friend and brother. I hope we can spend many more days together in the
wild and beautiful places of Kenya and Tanzania. Asante sana.*

Printed in Hong Kong through Bookbuilders Ltd.
91 92 93 94 95   5 4 3 2 1
Library of Congress Cataloging-in-Publication Data
Norton, Boyd.
The African elephant : last days of Eden / Boyd Norton.
p. cm.
Includes bibliographical references.
ISBN 0-89658-158-6
I. African elephant. 2. Endangered species—Africa, East. II. Title.
QL737.P98N69 1991

333.95'9—dc20

91-15075
CIP

Published by
Voyageur Press, Inc.
P.O. Box 338, 123 North Second Street
Stillwater, MN 55082 U.S.A.
From Minnesota and Canada 612-430-2210
Toll-free 800-888-9653

Voyageur Press books are also available at discounts for quantities for educational, fundraising, premium, or sales-promotion use. For details contact the marketing department. Please write or call for our free catalog of natural history publications.

CONTENTS

ACKNOWLEDGMENTS

Many people in Kenya and Tanzania took time from busy schedules to offer help in gathering material for this book. A special thanks to Richard Leakey, Cynthia Moss, Joyce Poole, Bill Woodley, Kuki Gallman, Ian and Jane Craig, Paul Chabeda, Abdi Omar Bashir, Iain and Oria Douglas-Hamilton, Daphne Sheldrick in Kenya. I'm indebted to Tanzania's David Babu, Isaac Muro, and Alfredo Pelizzoli.

I'm grateful for all the help in organizing my trips in East Africa, especially on the part of Dave Blanton, president of Voyagers International in Ithaca, New York, and Stephen Turner, director of East African Ornithological Safaris in Nairobi, Kenya. An additional thanks to Steve Turner, a fine wildlife photographer, for use of a couple of his pictures. Thanks, too, to Bill and Barbie Winter and Steve Austin of Bill Winter Safaris in Nairobi for their help and excellent safari service.

Thanks to writer Bob Jones for sharing notes and thoughts with me during the time we were on the assignment for *Audubon* magazine. Often, when I was busy photographing, my own notes were brief scribbles.

Les Line, the very talented and dedicated former editor of *Audubon* magazine, made it possible for me to gather much of the material for this book during a two-month-long assignment in 1990. (For those who don't know, Les Line, over his twenty-five-year tenure as editor, made *Audubon* one of the highest quality publications in the world.)

I'm very appreciative of the help given me by Diana McMeekin of the African Wildlife Foundation and Joyce Poole, Elephant Programme Coordinator for the Kenya Wildlife Service, both of whom took the time to read the manuscript and offer suggestions. Thanks, also, to the people at International Wildlife Coalition—Donna Hart, vice president, and Sharon Dunn-Smith.

As always I'm grateful for working with a fine bunch of people from Voyageur Press on this project and others—Helene Jones, my editor; Tom Lebovsky and Bob DuBois, publishers; Debbie Erickson, Kathy Mallien; and everyone else who had a hand in producing this book.

I would be remiss if I didn't give special thanks to some of East Africa's finest guides and drivers. Over the years, they have been responsible for introducing me to the wonders of Kenya and Tanzania. Without them I would have been lost—literally and figuratively. At East African Ornithological Safaris: David Ngunyi, Joseph Kabiru, Preston, Kitanyi, and Michael. In Tanzania: Msafiri Msury, Peter MacDougall, and Sengo Safaris. At the Mara River Camp: *Asante sana* to G. Micheu ("Mitch"), John, Obonyo, David, William, Vincent, Peter, and Peter.

Finally, my appreciation to the two people to whom this book is dedicated: John Lidede (who prefers just "Lidede") and Hussein Hamisi ("Husseini").

FOREWORD

Between 1979 and 1989, poaching for the ivory trade reduced Africa's elephant population from some 1.3 million to 609,000 individuals. Since the introduction of the international ban on trade in ivory in late 1989, the rate of poaching has declined significantly, giving many threatened populations of elephants a real chance for survival. The elephant has always been a favourite animal in the hearts and minds of people all over the world. Its great size, its many noble qualities and its highly complex social structure has endeared the elephant to many. It was the decision of millions of people around the world not to buy, wear or sell ivory that has made the ban such a success. The response of people has been extraordinary and the decline in the killing of elephants in Africa has demonstrated that individuals really can make a difference to the course of events on this planet. However, it is important for people not to view elephants as "saved," abandon them and move on to the next species. As the southern African countries continue to pressure for a reopening of the ivory trade, the protection of this highly intelligent species against man's greed for ivory will undoubtedly be an issue for many years to come. Elephants are going to need continued support from the public.

Despite our successes over the last two years, saving the elephant in the long-term still presents one of the greatest challenges to conservation in Africa. The issues surrounding the earth's largest land mammal are complex, particularly in areas where elephants have to compete with a growing human population for space to live. As elephants become confined to smaller protected areas they will present increasingly difficult dilemmas and decisions to wildlife managers. Against the background of the illegal killing of elephants for ivory, the possibility that places exist where there are too many elephants is often a difficult concept for people to understand.

Over the last few years many books have been written about the plight of the African elephant. In *The African Elephant: Last Days of Eden*, Boyd Norton provides the reader with great insight into the complex social world of elephants and the many challenges facing its survival. His clear and sensitive story, accompanied by beautiful photographs, takes the reader through some of the complex issues surrounding the conservation and management of elephants. He ends his story by pointing out simple but important ways for each one of us to help to save the African elephant.

—RICHARD E. LEAKEY, KENYA WILDLIFE SERVICE

INTRODUCTION

"Another book about elephants? Even you must be getting tired of the subject by now," commented a friend who knows well how deeply I have been immersed in the subject for the last several years. To the average citizen on the receiving end of direct mail appeals, it could easily seem that elephants have been studied and photographed and interpreted to such a degree that surely nothing is left to learn or to say. A cynic could even suggest that these wondrous animals are being exploited as a gimmick for enticing donations to wildlife foundations. Every time you turn around, there is a new book, article, or film about elephants.

Certainly the elephant has been the center of attention of late, and no doubt some of that attention reflects a "flavor of the month" approach to fundraising. But serious students of conservation know that however much attention is paid to elephants, including another book, it can never be too much. Only a few years ago, due to lack of attention, we came within a hair's breadth of letting the African elephant slide into extinction. We are just now beginning to halt that ominous slide.

Of course there were always a few inspired souls who paid a lot of attention to elephants. As early as the turn of the century, ivory hunters marveled at the intelligence of elephants. At Gangala na Bodio in what was then the Belgian Congo, officials proved that African elephants can be trained to be ridden just as Asian elephants can. And more recently, researchers such as AWF senior associate Iain and his wife Oria Douglas-Hamilton taught us of the animals' courage and magnanimity toward humans. Two other AWF senior associates, Cynthia Moss and Joyce Poole, have studied the elephants in Kenya's Amboseli National Park for many years. Moss has charted their complex family relationships from the basic mother-infant bond and the mother's closest female relatives to the distant cousins seen perhaps no more than once per year. Poole confirmed the presence of musth in African elephants — a condition previously thought to occur only in Asian elephants. And from the Amboseli Project comes the most startling news of all: The rumbling vibration early hunters called "boibirigmous" and imagined to be massive digestive tracts at work is actually elephantine conversation. Katherine Payne and Richard Langauer, working with Moss and Poole, have recorded these infrasonic rumbles. Enhanced play-backs have made it possible for the Amboseli team to recognize more than two dozen distinctive messages. We can only guess at how many will ultimately be identified.

Despite these pockets of deep interest and scholarship, little attention was paid to the plight of elephants continent-wide. But the poachers and ivory traders were paying attention to elephants and were waging an undeclared war to acquire ivory. Of course, some of the researchers tried to raise the alarm, but they were often ignored or dismissed as sentimental. There had always been so many elephants that it was inconceivable they could ever disappear. Those individuals with vested interest refuted the Cassandra-cries of the researchers and pointed out that the elephants destroy people's crops and lives. They pointed to the importance of the revenue that ivory sales brought to impoverished countries. Experts lectured, scientists argued, and governments dawdled while oil-importation costs went sky high, effective antipoaching patrols declined, guns left behind after civil wars proliferated, and all the while the elephants kept on dying and dying and dying.

In Amboseli park in Kenya, there is an elephant matriarch named Jezebel who has beaten incredible odds. When Jezebel was born in 1930, there were five to ten million elephants roaming the African continent. Think of it: five to ten million elephants only sixty years ago. In 1979, there were approximately 1.3 million, and in 1990 there were just over 600,000. Thousands of elephants are gone forever while, somehow, Jezebel came through it all. Jezebel is obviously one of the luckier ones, partly because she lives in Amboseli, which has suffered far less poaching than other parks, and because currently there is a ban on the international sale of ivory. But what if the countries involved meet again in Japan in 1992 and elect to lift the ban? How much longer would Jezebel's luck hold out?

That ban on ivory sales went into place because of education, because people began to listen and care and understand. Education is the way to ensure that people continue to care and to demand protection for the elephants. We have to understand even more about them in order to educate people — whose help is critical in ensuring elephants' survival into the next century.

"Another book about elephants" is exactly what we need.

— DIANA E. MCMEEKIN
AFRICAN WILDLIFE FOUNDATION

TSAVO

It is absurd for a man to kill an elephant. — Beryl Markham, *West With the Night*

*   *   *

Hiding in the scrub thornbush, they waited until near dusk. They knew that there was less likelihood of being spotted at this time of day by antipoaching forces in vehicles or by any of the patrolling aircraft. Such activities had increased enormously in the past few months, making their mission exceedingly perilous. But they were skilled at hiding in this hostile bush country of the Tsavo Plains. They were skilled, also, at survival. They were *shifta*. Their name had once meant "nomad" in their native Somali language, but it had become corrupted by transgressions of others and eventually came to mean "bandit." Now the term was synonymous with "poacher."

Moving slowly and crouching to keep a low profile, the five men began their stalk of the small herd of elephants. There was little breeze, but they checked carefully and often, making sure that they stayed upwind of the animals. Elephants are not poor of sight, but it is their sense of smell that is finely tuned and gives early warning of impending threats. These days, with many of their brethren being shot, the animals were jittery, testing the air frequently for any danger with upraised trunks.

There was still enough light in the western sky when the *shifta* made their move. Still crouched, they began sprinting toward the massive forms outlined ahead. When they were twenty yards from the elephants, one man stopped, stood erect, and raised the AK-47 rifle to his shoulder. He fired three times, in quick succession. The *pop-pop-pop* of the automatic weapon sounded innocently muffled. But the bullets had deadly impact.

The first elephant, brain shot, fell immediately in a cloud of powdery dust. The second, too, dropped quickly. But the third had been hit just behind the shoulder and ran screaming in fear and rage. The young bull elephant bolted almost a hundred yards from the other two before it staggered, dropped on its knees, and fell on its side. The *shifta* marksman had kept his weapon on single-fire mode. No need to waste bullets. And certainly no need to make too much noise. Besides, there was a certain pride of marksmanship here. Only fools and the unskilled spray bullets around indiscriminately.

The other elephants had fled, screaming and trumpeting into the descending night. They could be heard a long distance away, crashing through the brush. There was no point in pursuit. The men ran to the still warm carcasses and began working quickly. With axes and *pangas* they hacked away at flesh and bone to extract as much of the tusks as intact as possible. It was hard work, taking an hour or more before they stood with their curved prizes, gleaming in the pale light of a sliver of a moon. Then, with equal alacrity, they cut brush to cover the massive bodies. This would delay discovery by vultures, whose circling forms in the sky draw attention to death on the plains. The brush also would make difficult the detection of their deed by those aerial patrols over the park.

The men were tired when they finished, but there was no time for rest. They had to be at least twenty kilometers away before the light of dawn revealed

This youngster, probably a few weeks old, will be dependent on its mother's milk for about eighteen months before beginning to feed on vegetation.

their slaughter—in case anyone should discover it. Shouldering their booty, the men walked toward the east in single file. The last man carried a long branch with attached foliage, which he dragged along behind, switching it back and forth to obliterate their tracks. This would be necessary for the first kilometer or so of their trek; then they could ignore the erasure tactics and speed their pace.

With darkness the temperature plummeted. But the men, warmed by the exertion of carrying equipment plus almost twenty kilos of ivory, paid no mind. Only when they stopped for a quick rest did they shiver. Twenty kilos—about forty pounds. It was not a lot of ivory. Not like years past when one tusk might weigh forty kilos. But the big-tusked elephants were rare now, victims of other poachers like themselves. These would do, however. At a price of $250 a kilo on the world market, they had about $5,000 worth of ivory. But they would earn only about one-quarter of that from dealers which, divided five ways, would net each of them about $250. Back home in Somalia that was a year's wages, if anyone were lucky enough to find a job.

They pushed on through the darkness, stopping occasionally to rest, but only briefly. At dawn they would hide beneath a canopy of brush, probably in a place where they had cached food and water, and wait out the day's fiery heat and buzzing flies. Then at dusk again they would move on. They had a long way to go. A long way, indeed, across hellish brushlands where the dust burns the eyes. Their goal was a meeting place near where they had stashed other tusks. A truck would meet them, if it hadn't been intercepted by antipoaching patrols, on an obscure track. There they would transfer their booty plus the tusks from previous kills and receive payment. Then they would melt again into the brushlands and seek out more elephants, all the time at increasing risk of being spotted by the planes and helicopters and Land Rovers being used by the Kenyan antipoaching forces. If the armed poachers resisted, there would be no arrests, no prisons. The Kenyans had orders to shoot to kill. As they rested in the chilly night under the stars, they debated about taking their profits and leaving. The risks were becoming greater. It was a long way to that sailing dhow on the coast. Money was no good to a dead man. They continued on into the night.

* * *

I wheeled off the dusty road, up over the berm along the edge, and we went crashing through brush, stirring up clouds of red dust. Ahead of us the Land Rover with the antipoaching troops led the way, swerving around acacia trees and plowing through smaller bushes. Dust swirled in the windows and through the open top of our Suzuki. We debated about closing the roof hatch and windows, but the heat was fierce and we would have roasted. The midday sun in Tsavo is brutal. The whole land ahead of us swam in shimmering heat waves. The glare washed out all color, rendering everything pale and dry. Vegetation crackled under the tires.

I was with writer Bob Jones. The two of us were on assignment for *Audubon* magazine, he to write, and me to photograph the story of declining game in East Africa. As we swerved and bounced through the brush, Patrick Hamilton made one more pass over us in his Christen A-1 Husky STOL plane. Hamilton, formerly a senior game warden for Tsavo National Park, was now an antipoaching advisor and a reconnaissance pilot for the park. It was he who had set up this rendezvous with the antipoaching troops after he discovered the elephant bodies on a flight the day before.

For almost fifteen minutes we drove crazily across the searing landscape. We were about thirty yards from the carcasses when the stench of death hit us. At about the same time dozens of dark vultures rose ponderously into the air, spooked by the sound of the vehicles. The Land Rover stopped about twenty feet from the first elephant and I pulled up behind and switched off the engine. I was not anxious to get out.

They had been killed ten days, maybe two weeks earlier. The hides were desiccated, stained with the obscene white droppings of vultures and marabou storks, but the carcasses were still bulky and massive. In the stifling heat, the air was redolent with the sickening sweet odor of decaying flesh. Breathing through the mouth didn't help. Even more sickening was the fact that these once magnificent animals had been killed for their ivory—ivory that would find its way through a long, tortuous, and very lucrative path to the Kenya coast, then to Somalia, then by boat to the Far East, to Hong Kong or Singapore or Tokyo. And for what? These and other elephants were being slaughtered across Africa each year for carvings, for trinkets, for baubles to be sold in souvenir shops.

I circled the dead animals, photographing them

This lone bull may be approaching fifty years old. Elephants can live to sixty and possibly, under ideal conditions, seventy years old.

from every angle. I wanted these pictures to be shocking and disgusting, a strong visual message that, unless action is taken soon, we will lose one of the planet's most magnificent species. I was also nervous, apprehensive. I was glad we had waited for the antipoaching troops to accompany us, for often the *shifta* will stash the tusks of a recent kill and stay in an area to continue their savage depredations. It would have been dangerous for Bob and me to be here alone. Only two weeks earlier, in a private reserve in another part of Kenya, we had stumbled on a freshly killed rhino with its horn cut off. I began photographing it and suddenly had this chilling sensation that I was being watched—perhaps through a gunsight. We got the hell out of there, but not before I got more pictures.

I moved in close to the elephants, unpleasant though it was, to be sure to capture on film the horror of a once magnificent animal with its face and jaw hacked away. I wanted people to be shocked at the real price of buying trinkets of ivory. Several rolls of film later, when I had finished, I simply stood and looked. It was a sight I will never forget.

As we drove off, I looked back once more. Vultures circled, twenty or more of them, and some had returned to the bodies even before we were out of sight. Within a week the scavengers would reduce the elephants to a pile of bones and a few ragged patches of leathery hide. In a couple of years even these remains might be gone, picked at, scoured by insects, decayed and eroded by water and blistering sun, covered by blowing sand. Gone. But I vowed that these photographic images would be used to help keep remaining elephants alive by serving as a reminder of the price of greed and stupidity.

*   *   *

Tsavo. This was the first park I visited several years ago on my first trip to East Africa. I can still remember the excitement of that safari. The first one is always the most vivid, although others remain etched indelibly in memory.

All the magical qualities of East Africa come together here in Kenya's Tsavo National Park: vast, open spaces of scrub-brush savannah swimming in heat waves of midday sunlight; rocky hills with tall, elegant giraffes lumbering among grass-choked boulders; sculpted, graceful forms of acacia trees spreading their umbrellas of thorns and leaves over grazing Thomson's and Grant's gazelles; and red lateritic earth that distinguishes Tsavo from other areas of Kenya. When Tsavo elephants dust themselves or spray themselves with mud from waterholes, as elephants do, they take on a distinctive red color that is so different from the gray or muddy brown color of elephants in Amboseli or Masai Mara as to make them appear to be a distinctly different species.

I remember, too, my first Tsavo sunrise, seen from atop the cliffs at Roaring Rocks in Tsavo West. The sun blasted up over the distant horizon formed by those plains that go on forever, flat and endless in their reach, all the way to the warm waters of the Indian Ocean coast and the white beaches of Mombasa. There is a quality of light here in East Africa, and especially at Tsavo, that I've never found anywhere else in my travels. Perhaps it's minute dust particles in the air. Or maybe it's the clarity of the air that lends itself, in prismatic ways, to making sunlight do wondrous things.

I stood shivering in the dim predawn light. Somewhere below, in that *nyika* (wilderness) of scrub-brush and acacia, a hyena made its musical *whooup, whooup* call. I heard, or thought I heard, the bellowing roar of a lion far off. (What else, I thought; this is, after all, called Roaring Rocks.) I was glad my guide, Lidede, was keeping a sharp eye on things while I prepared to photograph the sunrise.

It was not a disappointing sunrise—it rarely is in East Africa. All the brilliance and all the color were there, captured somewhat imprecisely on film. But as the sun rose higher and began to illuminate the landscape below, I noticed some movement. Four massive forms lumbered across a grassy swale, seemingly at our feet. Elephants! "*Tembo wakubwa,*" whispered Lidede. Big elephants. Later I learned that the sound I had mistaken for a lion's roar could well have come from the elephants. Often they make a rumbling sound of such timbre that it does, indeed, seem to be a distant roar. Subsequently, in other places, I've heard it and continue to be fooled.

As I looked out on the dawn over this primal landscape, I felt that I was watching the dawn of the world. My whole psyche became transported to the early Pleistocene. Africa can do that to you. Instead of standing there with camera and tripod, I could well have been holding a crude spear, dressed in skins. The fear and apprehension are real. It is a savage world out there, still. But it's also a world filled with savage splendor. One wonders if our pre-

Male elephants usually spend their time in solitude, although they sometimes travel with a few other bachelors. They are never far from family units led by females.

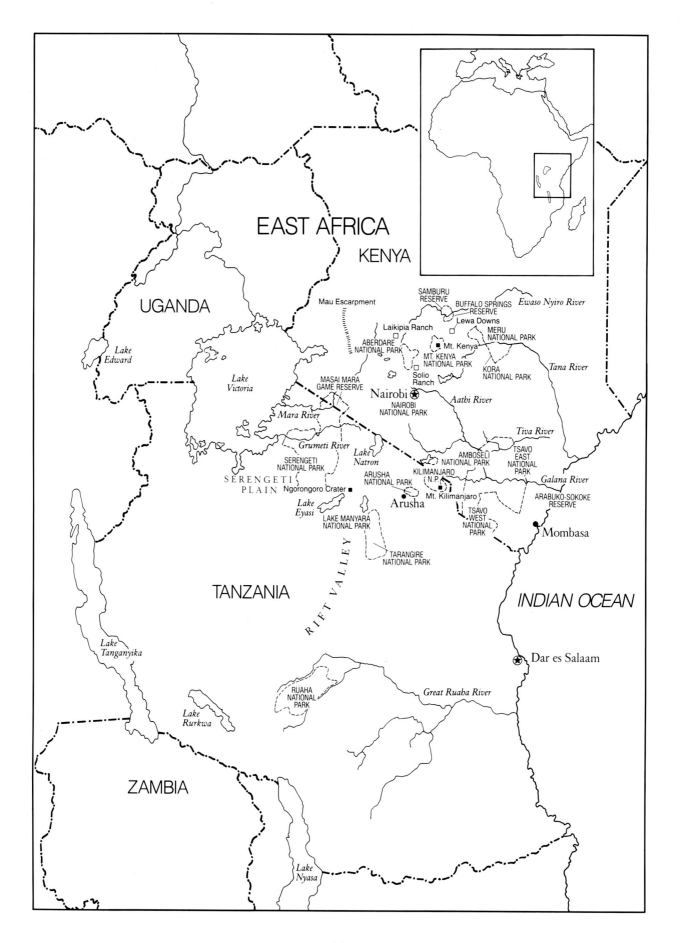

EAST AFRICA

KENYA

UGANDA

Lake Edward

Lake Victoria

Mau Escarpment

SAMBURU RESERVE
BUFFALO SPRINGS RESERVE
Lewa Downs
Ewaso Nyiro River

Laikipia Ranch

ABERDARE NATIONAL PARK
MT. KENYA NATIONAL PARK
■ Mt. Kenya
MERU NATIONAL PARK

Solio Ranch
KORA NATIONAL PARK
Tana River

MASAI MARA GAME RESERVE

Nairobi ✪
NAIROBI NATIONAL PARK
Aathi River

Mara River

Tiva River

Grumeti River

SERENGETI NATIONAL PARK

Lake Natron

AMBOSELI NATIONAL PARK
TSAVO EAST NATIONAL PARK

SERENGETI PLAIN

ARUSHA NATIONAL PARK
KILIMANJARO N.P.

Ngorongoro Crater ■

Galana River

Lake Eyasi

● Mt. Kilimanjaro
Arusha ●

LAKE MANYARA NATIONAL PARK

TSAVO WEST NATIONAL PARK

ARABUKO-SOKOKE RESERVE

● Mombasa

TARANGIRE NATIONAL PARK

TANZANIA

RIFT VALLEY

INDIAN OCEAN

Lake Tanganyika

Dar es Salaam ✪

RUAHA NATIONAL PARK

Great Ruaha River

Lake Rurkwa

ZAMBIA

Lake Nyasa

historic forebears stopped now and then to marvel at the beauty of a dawn sky and the awesome majesty of elephants.

* * *

Tsavo first achieved notoriety during the building of the Mombasa-Uganda Railway in 1898, for it was the locale of the infamous "Man-eaters of Tsavo," lions that killed nearly one hundred of the workers on the line. While building the bridge to span the Tsavo River, hundreds of Indian laborers were encamped north of the present-day town of Voi. Two large and *kali* lions had developed a taste for human flesh, and, periodically, marauded the camps, stealing into carefully guarded *bomas* at night and dragging off from their tents screaming victims. For eight months the cats, through luck and cunning, eluded hunters and guards. They were even bold enough to break into railroad cars for their prey. The terror brought work on the railroad to a halt, but eventually the man-eaters were killed and the work resumed. Even today, it is said that lions of Tsavo are particularly bold.

For ivory hunters, the Tsavo Plains were a paradise because elephants were numerous. When records were first made of such things, it was estimated that the elephant population in the Tsavo region was more than forty thousand. And, most important, Tsavo elephants tended to be heavier-tusked than those of other regions. Moreover, Tsavo is not far from the coast where the ivory could be shipped to those lucrative foreign markets.

The hunters profited from East Africa's climate. During and after the rainy season, elephants and other animals are dispersed over wide areas, because green forage and water are abundant. But with the fiery heat of the dry season, leaves and grasses become desiccated, brown and dry and of little nutritional value to the grazers and browsers. Water evaporates from the waterholes and intermittent river courses like the Tiva dry up, becoming rivers of sand. The game is forced to migrate to the permanent sources of water: the Galana, the Athi, and the Tsavo rivers (the Athi and Tsavo join to form the Galana). During the prolonged drought the animals never stray far from these river corridors, making it easier for hunters and poachers to find their prey.

Until there was a market for ivory, it's doubtful that early African hunters had much impact on elephant populations. It was particularly dangerous to attempt to kill an elephant with primitive weapons.

Other, less dangerous game was abundant.

With British colonization of Kenya in the late nineteenth century came an increase in big game hunting as a sport. By the 1930s there were numerous "great white hunters" who guided rich clientele on game-hunting safaris. Tsavo was one of the popular areas, particularly for hunting elephants. Baron Bror von Blixen, husband of Karen Blixen, pioneered some tracks into the hitherto trackless expanse of Tsavo's *nyika* to lead his hunting clientele on safaris. And Denys Finch-Hatton, Karen Blixen's paramour, led hunting safaris in Tsavo before his tragic death in an airplane crash at Voi.

The participants in these safaris were trophy hunters, seeking the biggest and the best of the species they slaughtered. Just any elephant would not do. It had to be the biggest bull with the biggest tusks; one hundred kilo tuskers were the goal, that is, elephants with tusks weighing a total of at least one hundred kilos, or 220 pounds. To aid in successful hunting, von Blixen and Finch-Hatton and others enlisted the aid of new technology—the airplane. Finch-Hatton was a pilot, and von Blixen, on occasion, called upon Beryl Markham to fly over the vastness of Tsavo to scout the locale of the biggest tuskers. Though she loved flying and loved the adventure of scouting out new territory from the air, Beryl Markham had mixed feelings about elephant hunting, as she wrote in her classic book, *West With the Night:*

It is absurd for a man to kill an elephant. It is not brutal, it is not heroic, and certainly it is not easy; it is just one of those preposterous things that men do like putting a dam across a great river.

This was sport hunting, as opposed to poaching. According to the white hunters, sport hunting was good. Poaching was bad. The distinction, clearly, was not evident to many of the native people who lived in the region, for along with the increase in hunting came a marked increase in ivory poaching, driven by the slowly increasing price of ivory.

* * *

Tsavo National Park was established in 1948. The two units, Tsavo East and Tsavo West, total over eight thousand square miles in area, making it Kenya's largest park and one of the largest in Africa. (For comparison, Yellowstone National Park is 3,400 square miles in area, making Tsavo over two and a third times larger.) The park status made the killing of any animals within park boundaries illegal.

Frank William Woodley, known as "Bill" and, sometimes, "Billy" to his friends, was one of the first two wardens appointed to the new Tsavo National Park. Actually, his title was "junior assistant warden," but since there were only three people, including his superior, the warden, to patrol eight thousand square miles of wilderness, the titles didn't seem to matter. It was April 1948. Bill Woodley was nineteen years old. For the next four decades, his life was inextricably linked to Tsavo and Tsavo's elephants.

Bill's first assignment was to explore the vast and nearly trackless expanse of Tsavo East, that area lying east of the infamous Mombasa/Nairobi railroad line. The other junior assistant warden, Peter Jenkins, was given Tsavo West. The two were instructed to make records of all species of animals and birds observed on their exploration and, where possible, to begin marking park boundaries.

Despite his tender years, Woodley was an experienced hunter and had taken numerous trophy tusks in Tanganyika and Mozambique. He had considered becoming a professional hunter, leading plush safaris, but already he was sickened by the killing of animals, particularly elephants. Thus, despite the low pay, the job at Tsavo National Park was an exciting prospect, allowing him to be in the wilds with the animals he loved without having to participate in the slaughter of these animals. And so, with a local assistant and a beat up old truck, Woodley left on his trek feeling greatly exhilarated. When he returned two weeks later from this preliminary foray, he was dismayed.

What Bill had to report to his superior, senior warden Ronald Stevens, was the discovery of extensive poaching activities in his area of the park. In all he had found nineteen dead elephants and four dead rhino, and that was in a relatively small area of the park that he had managed to cover. Moreover, it appeared that the poachers did their work with bows and arrows.

Chief warden Stevens was skeptical, particularly about the primitive weapons used. It was unlikely that a single arrow could bring down such a massive beast as an elephant. It was true that some hunters had developed poisons from natural plants, but they would have to be extremely potent to kill an elephant or a rhino. No, it just didn't seem likely. Per-

haps Woodley's youth and inexperience clouded his judgment and accuracy of observation.

Over the next few months Woodley returned to the bush with Elui, a local Kamba tracker and hunter now hired as his ranger. As before, he was pushing tracks into the *nyika* and marking park boundaries. But he was also finding increasing evidence of poaching on a massive scale.

One evening around a campfire, Elui explained to Woodley that poaching had become a way of life for certain native people in the region. As he explained it, there was a well-organized industry, a network ranging from the hunters themselves to the poison suppliers to the dealers on the coast who bought the ivory. There were even brewers who made palm wine to sell to the hunters who happily celebrated their hunts with the potent concoction. It appeared that this had been going on for decades and, to varying degrees, perhaps even for a hundred years — or at least for as long as there has been a market for ivory.

The hunters were the Liangulu who, for some strange reason, specialized in killing nothing but elephants, save for an occasional rhino whose horn was valuable. The Liangulu used an extremely powerful bow called the Big Bow. The Big Bow required an enormous pull, a force of over one hundred pounds in most cases, which meant that the arrow was delivered with great power behind it.

However powerful the bow, it is nearly impossible to bring down an elephant with an arrow alone unless the hunter is accurate enough to hit a vital organ. And so to add to the killing power, the Liangulu applied a potent poison to the arrow's tip and shaft, a lethal toxin called *hada*.

The production of *hada* was a specialized industry of the Giriama people who live near the coast, east of Tsavo. Though they rarely used the poison themselves, the Giriama had developed the method of producing *hada* over many generations, and the formulas, carefully guarded secrets, were handed down through families. The primary ingredient comes from the bark and branches of the acokanthera, a bushy tree with dark green leaves and aromatic white flowers. The branches, sliced into small pieces, are boiled in water for hours and periodically replaced by fresh pieces. Other ingredients are added, some chosen for magical, rather than toxic qualities. The resultant tarlike mass is packed in leaves and sold to the hunters who apply it carefully to arrow shafts and tips in a prescribed manner. So

A stack of three thousand tusks, confiscated from poachers, was worth an estimated $3 million. In July 1989, Kenya's President Daniel arap Moi set a torch to this pile. (Photo © by Steve Turner)

potent is this poison that only two milligrams—a quantity the size of a pin head—can kill an average-sized man in minutes. There is no known antidote.

Even with a well-placed shot with a Liangulu arrow, it often took hours for an elephant to die—a slow, painful death for the animal. Sometimes it took days.

To Woodley's horror, he discovered the extent of poaching activity in Tsavo and surrounding regions to the east. There were hundreds involved, mostly Liangulu. An estimated several hundred elephants were killed each year and in some years it may have reached a thousand or more.

When his superiors finally realized that it was a serious situation, Woodley was given authority to bring the poaching to a halt. For the next nine years Woodley and others relentlessly tracked down the Liangulu hunters and arrested them and others associated with the poaching network, including certain ivory merchants on the coast. It was an incredible task, carried out mostly in the blazing wilderness of Tsavo East. Equally incredible was the care and tact used by Woodley. Often he convinced the captured poachers to reform and to work for him in tracking and catching others. Many obliged, becoming valuable assistants.

By the end of 1957 it was possible for park officials to declare that poaching in Tsavo was virtually eliminated. But Tsavo's, and Woodley's, problems were far from over.

In the early 1960s there was a measurable increase in the population of elephants in the Tsavo region. To the east of the park, in a three-thousand-square-mile reserve called Galana Ranch, elephant population was also growing. The increase in the number of elephants began to affect the habitat. After a series of droughts and fires, the situation became critical. The woodland of the region was being destroyed by hungry elephants, particularly those areas near permanent water sources where elephants and other animals were forced, by drought, to congregate. As woodland was destroyed, it was replaced by grasslands. But this habitat change created problems for other species as well. Rhinos, in particular, are sensitive to alteration of their environment. Being browsers, they live in the kind of brushy country found in the mixed woodlands. Rhinos, however, don't adapt to grasslands, and thus park officials noted a decline in rhino populations.

Whether the halt of poaching was responsible for an increase in elephant population is still uncertain,

though it's likely that it contributed some part. It's also likely that elephant migration into the park was a contributor. More and more surrounding areas were being farmed and settled by an increasing human population, forcing elephants to leave former habitat and seek sanctuaries free of human harassment.

By the early 1960s, the concept of "game management" was becoming popular, if not trendy, among the wildlife and park administrators of East Africa. The idea is to harvest "surplus" wild animals, thus maintaining optimal populations for a given habitat. The Galana Game Management Scheme, begun in 1958, was to carry out this idea in practice. Since this area was outside the national park, the killing could be done without violating the park's no-hunting mandate. Furthermore, the scheme of shooting "surplus" elephants was to be carried out by former Liangulu poachers and others in a kind of make-work project for out-of-work poachers now being released after serving their prison sentences. It's understandable that these former poachers were incredulous at the idea. When they killed elephants it was bad. Now that white wardens wanted to kill elephants, with their help, it was good. Small wonder that, within another two decades, poaching would become rampant again.

The Galana Game Management Scheme was hardly a success. Enough forest habitat remained for the elephants to find shelter from the hunters. A few hundred were killed, but soon the remainder moved out of the area, some moving into Tsavo National Park to seek refuge from bullets.

By the late 1960s and early 1970s the situation in Tsavo was critical. Most of the forest country was destroyed, and periodic drought, together with lack of food, was causing the death of more and more elephants. Emaciated elephants bewilderedly wandered among bare stumps and snags of dead trees, a landscape that looked as though it had been victim of wartime bombing raids.

Amid this crisis it was proposed that five thousand elephants in Tsavo be shot to allow the habitat to recover. Immediately there was an international outcry by conservationists against this policy, particularly since it was against the very rules governing national parks—that there be no killing of animals in such sanctuaries. Bill Woodley was quoted as saying, "Hell, it's a bloody farce. Here we'd been jailing Liangulu for killing the animals, and now, a few years later, we are wanting to annihilate five thousand—and in a game sanctuary!" The scheme was never carried out, but the elephant overcrowding did not go away.

In 1971 an estimated nine thousand elephants died in Tsavo East and West National Parks. Some thought the number might have been closer to fifteen thousand. Severe drought continued until 1976, and Tsavo's landscape resembled that of a desert rather than the former rich mixture of grass and woodland. Bones of dead elephants were scattered over wide areas. But in this parched landscape there were signs already of change: Seedlings of new trees were struggling against the dehydrated soil and the blazing sun. When the rains came in 1976, they were not heavier than they had been in normal years, but they began to add the needed moisture back to this desiccated land.

The huge die-off of elephants naturally attracted some of the native people who lived nearby, for there was ivory everywhere to be found and retrieved and sold. No illegal hunting was required. However, when this easy supply ran out, many took to hunting. A new wave of poaching began.

The new poachers found their task somewhat easier than it had been in the past. The forest cover was now gone over most areas, making it difficult for elephants to hide from their pursuers. By 1974 more elephants were being slaughtered by poaching than by drought or starvation. And by the beginning of the 1980s, ivory prices were increasing, fueling more intensive poaching.

The new wave of elephant hunters were not armed with *hada*-tipped arrows. They were now using new, more efficient technology—high-powered firearms. They also had vehicles to travel long distances and transport ivory. In addition, the Somalis, who have always claimed that northeastern Kenya was traditionally a part of Somalia, moved into the region and soon became efficient and deadly poachers.

The same drought that had affected Tsavo and environs had had devastating impact on Somalia. Nearly two million cattle, sheep and goats of the pastoralist tribes died. In desperation, many of these people migrated into parts of adjacent Kenya and Ethiopia seeking work and sustenance. But there was little legal work for them. As these *shifta* spread out from border areas, into the interior of Kenya, they moved into regions of the Tana and Galana Rivers. There they found elephants and rhinos that could be killed for great profit. Moreover, these *shif-*

ta were not adverse to eliminating their competition, local hunters, from time to time, particularly since it seemed to reinforce Somalia's claim to these lands. Tsavo became both an ecological and a political battlefield.

Bill Woodley's exemplary work had been rewarded in 1959 by promotion to chief warden of the Kenya Mountain National Parks, which included Mt. Kenya and the Aberdares and, eventually, Marsabit, Lake Nakuru, and Mt. Elgon. Thus he was not in the Tsavo area at this time of terrible slaughter and death by drought and starvation. But in 1978 Woodley was pressed into antipoaching service once again and, for three months, directed operations to clear out poachers from Tsavo. The actions were successful, temporarily, despite severely limited funding available.

In 1983 Woodley was appointed wildlife advisor to Kenya's park authorities. Already there were signs once again that poaching countrywide was on the increase. The price of ivory had jumped significantly, and stories circulated about new, well-organized bands of poachers at work. Not all, it seems, were *shifta*. There were widespread rumors of *magendo* (corruption) in the parks and wildlife departments. With ivory commanding a high price, money was available for bribing park rangers and wardens to look the other way. Some said that rangers even participated in poaching themselves, tempted because of meager salaries. Even worse were allegations that highly placed officials were involved in the poaching network.

By 1989 poaching had once again reached crisis proportions. The slaughter of Tsavo elephants alone was estimated to be more than a thousand a year. A census in 1988 revealed a population of less than 5,500 elephants in Tsavo and surrounding areas. At that rate of killing, Tsavo would have no more elephants by 1994 or sooner.

The poachers had become more sophisticated than ever and were well organized into a Mafia-like network. Using vehicles and radio communication, together with automatic weapons and chainsaws, they could strike fast, kill their prey, cut out the tusks, and be on their way before antipoaching forces could respond. The smuggling of ivory became equally sophisticated. In some cases aircraft were used to move tusks out of an area. Sometimes tusks were cached, then moved in one big batch using such things as false-bottomed oil tanker trucks.

This time it seemed like the last big push for the

February 1990 in Tsavo East National Park. I was with a ranger from the Tsavo Anti-Poaching Unit. These elephants were killed by poachers about ten days before these photos were taken. This is the real price of buying ivory trinkets.

Bill Woodley and Paul Chabeda, assistant director of Kenya Wildlife Service, look over some tusks confiscated from poachers in Tsavo National Park.

Antipoaching rangers on practice maneuvers in Tsavo West National Park, Kenya. Some still use older model British Enfield rifles, but these are being replaced by new G-3 automatic weapons.

poachers. The eradication of the elephant from Kenya, from Tsavo in particular, was a horrifyingly real prospect. As worldwide attention became focused on conservation efforts here, Kenya's President, Daniel arap Moi, made some bold moves to thwart the ivory poachers. In April 1989 he appointed Richard Leakey as head of Kenya's Wildlife Service. The son of famed archaeologists Louis S. B. and Mary Leakey, and a native Kenyan, Richard had become a noted archaeologist in his own right. His discoveries at Koobie Fora on Lake Turkana's shores had proven to be as earth shaking to the archaeological world as his parents'.

Leakey wasted no time in setting a course of action. One of his first acts as director was to call Bill Woodley. "Billy, can you clear up this situation in Tsavo?" he asked the antipoaching veteran. Woodley's answer was as direct as always: "Yes, I can clear it up."

Moi's appointment of Leakey restored confidence in the wildlife services department. Leakey reached out worldwide for help and soon had equipment donated to the cause: new Land Rovers, airplanes for aerial reconnaissance, even the loan of British

SAS (Special Air Services—a Delta Task Force--type organization) helicopters for staging raids. New G-3 automatic weapons replaced ancient rifles. Woodley took over the job of training and recruiting Kenya's Anti-Poaching Unit (APU), with headquarters in Tsavo. There were new uniforms and better salaries for the men. Also, there was money available for Woodley to use in paying informants—a good incentive for locals to give information on recent whereabouts of the *shifta*.

The new get-tough policy began to have an immediate impact. President Moi issued a shoot-to-kill order for poachers. In July of 1989 Leakey arranged for a media event to demonstrate to the world the seriousness of Kenya in halting the slaughter: President Moi personally touched off the massive blaze that destroyed a twelve-ton mountain of confiscated ivory valued at over $3 million.

*　　*　　*

I sat with Bill Woodley on the terrace of the Voi Safari Lodge, drinking Tusker beer. The label on the bottle depicted an elephant, ears flared and trunk raised high, with a set of big tusks. Over the railing

Antipoaching rangers on patrol in Tsavo East National Park, Kenya.

24

Sign on the road between Tsavo West and Amboseli national parks, Kenya. Perhaps there ought to be one for elephants: BEWARE OF HUMANS — They Can Be Dangerous to Your Health.

of the terrace and about one hundred feet below was a water hole. Several dusty red elephants stood around it drinking. None had tusks like the ones on the bottle.

"They stay near the lodges now," Bill said. "They feel safer." Sitting with us were a television producer and reporter, lovely young ladies who might have graced the pages of a fashion magazine. They were from a Santiago, Chile, television station. It was February 1990, and elephant poaching was a big story worldwide. Earlier that afternoon I had photographed the three dead elephants.

Bill answered the reporter's questions, then they moved over to the edge of the terrace so he could be interviewed on camera, with Tsavo's vast plains, and perhaps those elephants, as a background. He was used to such interviews. I thought about my first meeting with Bill, in September of 1989, not many months after he took over antipoaching training at Leakey's request. He showed me the trainees at Manyani, not far from here in Tsavo West, and some of the new equipment. Bill expressed great hope that these troops would bring the poaching to a halt, not only here but in other areas of Kenya. Bill

had been fighting poachers for forty-one years.

Between that trip in September and this one, the Convention on International Trade in Endangered Species (CITES) had met in Lausanne, Switzerland, and most nations of the world signed a treaty banning the sale of ivory in the United States, European countries, and many other nations. (South Africa, Zimbabwe, and Botswana did not sign. The three nations profit from ivory sales and from the continued sale of very expensive hunting licenses — $30,000 a crack — sold mostly to rich Americans who come to shoot elephants.) Now, I was told in February, the price of ivory was already dropping drastically. For how long, no one knew.

The battle rages. Eighteen poachers had been killed at the time of my February visit. And there are signs that poaching is tapering off. Everyone is hopeful, but everyone agrees that as long as there are people foolish enough to buy ivory and as long as there is poverty, people will be tempted to risk their lives for the profit.

And there are three new dead elephants out there to prove it.

Overleaf: This family in Tsavo East National Park acted very jittery when we approached in a vehicle, testing the air nervously with their trunks. It was an obvious sign that they had been witnesses to poaching activity in the area.

A calf suckles while its mother continues feeding. This youngster may be about one year old.

DAYS OF EDEN

A glorious scene. It seemed, from hundreds of buffaloes, zebras and lordly elephants feeding majestically, to be like what must have been seen by angels when megatheria fed undisturbed in primeval forests. — David Livingstone, 1856, *The Last Journals of David Livingstone in Central Africa*

*   *   *

The African elephant is descended from ancestors that roamed the earth more than forty million years ago, a time when our ancestors still lived in trees. Because modern survivors of elephants fall into two groups, the African and the Indian elephants, it's easy to assume that all progenitors of elephants were confined to Africa and India. However, elephantids, large mammals with trunks and tusks and bearing close resemblance to today's species, were found almost worldwide at one time—from Africa to Europe, from Asia to North and South America. In fact, only ten thousand years ago, at the end of the last Ice Age, there were three species of elephantids in North America: the tundra wooly mammoth found in the far north, the grazing mammoth of warmer grasslands, and the American mastodont found in woodlands. There's strong evidence that all three of these species became extinct because of the skills of early hunters in North America.

When the dinosaurs died off suddenly and mysteriously, near the end of the Cretaceous Period some sixty-five million years ago, ecological niches opened up for other species to fill. Mammals had already existed since the early Triassic, 250 million years ago. But because reptiles had developed so prolifically and efficiently and ruled the land, mammals remained small and secretive, like rodents, living on vegetation or insects and staying out of the way of larger critters.

After the disappearance of the dinosaurs, mammals flourished. The new and diverse species slowly evolved and claimed newly available habitats. It was no longer necessary to remain small and secretive in order to survive, and the mammals' larger sizes and longer legs empowered them with greater mobility and, thus, the capability of ranging over larger areas to take advantage of food. This was especially beneficial to the herbivores, the grazers and browsers, for it meant that these animals could move on when their food supply became overgrazed.

The increased size of mammals also protected them; it was harder to be preyed upon by predators. Size, in other words, became a defense. But increasing size brought with it new problems, such as obtaining and processing enough food. As the herbivores grew in size, so did their need to eat more and to eat more efficiently. Teeth became flattened and enlarged to grind more vegetation. In some cases, certain teeth became enlarged, as tusks, to help strip, gouge, or displace vegetation, though in most cases tusks later were used more for defense or dominance display.

The increase in size of certain mammals brought with it the need for structural change as well. Because of greater body mass, thicker, stronger legs were required to support the weight. Where not only body mass increased, but height as well, other problems developed. A tall mammal must have a reasonable means to drink water. One way to do this is to develop a long neck and a small head, to reach water easily — a large, massive head on a long neck would be difficult to support. As an alternative, the animal could drop to its knees for a drink, though this would leave it vulnerable, and with such great mass, a lot of energy is expended in returning to standing position. Some massive species, like the rhinoceros, solved the problem by maintaining short, stubby legs so its head was close to water. But greater height gives opportunity to browse on a greater variety of vegetation—trees, for example. In the case of elephantids, gradual evolutionary change resulted in development of a trunk, a wonderful organ that aids both in food gathering in hard-to-reach places, and in getting a drink when the head is so far above the water source.

The late Eocene Epoch, about forty million years ago, marks the emergence of the order Proboscidea to which modern-day elephants belong. These early species bore little resemblance to today's elephants, looking more like small hippos. But they marked the beginning of an evolutionary change that brought about larger sized bodies and the gradual development of tusks and trunks. By the late Miocene, or eight to ten million years ago, one species, *Primelephas,* lived in East Africa in savannah lands not unlike the region today. Though this species eventually died out, archaeologists and zoologists recognize *Primelephas* as the progenitor of the three families of elephantids that emerged in modern times: *Loxodonta,* from which modern African elephants are descended; *Elephas,* from which the Indian elephant springs; and *Mammuthus,* which led to the mammoths of Europe and North America that became extinct not so very long ago.

When we think about the ecosystems that existed long ago, before the emergence of modern humans, there's a tendency to think of it all as Eden, where life went on uncomplicated and peacefully. But things were rarely peaceful for long. Geologic changes were sometimes abrupt and damaging. Climatic cycles brought conditions that made life tougher for some species and easier for others. The key condition is not stasis, but change. Vegetation grows. Herbivores eat the vegetation. Predators eat the herbivores. When climate or geologic forces cause change, new ecological relationships emerge. Old species die out, new ones take their place. And so it goes.

While it's true that change is inherent in ecosystems, these modifications generally take place slowly, over eons. The savannahs and the climate of East Africa have remained little changed now for the past two million years. And the ways of the elephants seen today roaming the forest-and-woodland habitat of Tsavo or Tarangire or Masai Mara are not much different from their ancestors' ways of two million years ago.

*   *   *

Elephant life revolves around the matriarchal family unit, which forms the core of existence and survival for all members, both male and female. The family unit also provides the environment for experiential learning for the offspring, behavior and knowledge passed on from generation to generation, such as knowing how and where to dig for water in certain dried-up streambeds during time of drought.

The leader of the family unit is usually the oldest female, the matriarch with many years' experience and knowledge. She is the memory bank and the teacher, gradually imparting to others such things as where to find certain browse at certain seasons, and determining how serious a threat a human or animal might be. Other members of the group defer to her judgment in time of stress or threat, fleeing when she gives the signal or standing ground threateningly, even charging, when she deems it necessary.

The unit is comprised of mothers and daughters of various ages, together with males that have not yet reached puberty. Daughters often will remain with the family unit for all of their lives, but males leave when they reach puberty—about twelve to fourteen years of age.

The size of family units can range from just two, a female with a youngster, to a group of a dozen or more. They move about together, never separated by any great distance for any great length of time. If there has been much successful breeding and the family unit becomes too large—when the unit exceeds twenty or so in number—it may split and form two separate family units. The splinter group may be small, with perhaps one or two females and their young. The split may be gradual, and even after the new group has become independent of the first, the two units maintain a close relationship and visit with each other often.

There is strong bonding in a family. Members of the family help each other during times of stress or difficulty. The rearing of youngsters is a shared responsibility. Often, lactating females will suckle youngsters that are not their own. Family members also will go to the aid of sick or injured kin.

Elephants graze in the arid country of Buffalo Springs National Reserve in northern Kenya. Mt. Kenya, or "Kirinyaga" in the Kikuyu language, 17,165 feet in elevation, is in the background.

Overleaf: A family group grazes in lush grasses while a dust devil swirls in the dry, arid portion of Amboseli National Park.

At birth, an elephant weighs about 250 pounds and is a little under three feet in height, a tiny, delicate creature compared to the massive adults. Though it can walk, somewhat shakily, shortly after it is born, the infant is helpless and totally dependent on adult care, provided by the mother and aunts and older siblings. For the first two years of its life, it depends entirely on its mother's milk for nourishment. The youngster is vulnerable to predation by lions or hyenas, and the family unit provides the needed protection.

The first year of a youngster's life is a period of intense learning. First an elephant has to learn to use that strange appendage attached to its face. From the start, it's an impediment; the infant often trips over its own unwieldy trunk. Learning to drink water with it is a process that requires practice. Sucking in too much fills the nasal cavities, causing a fit of sneezing. But at times it's a comfort. Sometimes a youngster sucks its trunk like a human infant sucks its thumb.

In addition to family units, there are also bond-groups made up of separate, and often related, family units. When a dozen or more family units get together to form a bond-group, the congregation can be quite large, sometimes numbering two hundred or more. It's not clear why such bond-groups are formed, and perhaps bond-groups serve more than survival purposes. Being social animals, elephants seem to enjoy the company of their kin. At times when the family units join together, it is with much excitement and greeting, with upraised heads and tails and trumpeting and touching with trunks, sometimes accompanied by copious urination. These large groups will sometimes stay together for weeks, moving over an area and feeding. Eventually the family units split off to wander their own way, and the bond-group breaks up. Often, however, these individual family units range within communication distance of each other, though staying separate.

There are uncounted stories of elephants coming to the aid of comrades, sometimes using tusks and trunks in an attempt to lift wounded or sick family members to their feet. One former Kenyan game warden told of an incident in which he had to shoot an elephant that had been raiding crops in a farm. He killed the animal near its forest domain and immediately other family members rushed up to help the stricken elephant. It had been a clean kill and the elephant fell in a heap near where it had been hit. The

other elephants crowded around in alarm and tried to raise their fallen comrade. One, with large tusks, lowered her head and shoved the tusks under the massive body, then attempted to lift it. The strain was so great that one of the tusks snapped off with a loud crack and spiraled through the air for a dozen yards. But this did not stop her efforts at moving her fallen kin. She and the other family members milled about for an hour or more before realizing that there was nothing they could do. They moved off into the forest, but it was reported that for the next two days they returned frequently to check on the slain animal.

*   *   *

The legend of the elephant graveyard, where old elephants go to die, leaving a fortune of ivory to be discovered, is simply not true. However, elephants seem to have a fascination with death. Iain Douglas-Hamilton, noted for his elephant research at Lake Manyara in Tanzania, recorded several instances of elephants becoming excited by, and perhaps even obsessed with, dead brethren, whether related or not. On discovering the bones of a dead elephant, family members examined them carefully, rolling them over, picking them up in their trunks, even putting them in their mouths. On a couple of occasions the elephants carried off tusks and bones and deposited them in nearby brush. Other observers have reported, on numerous occasions, that elephants have buried or covered bones of dead elephants and other animals. There was even a case of a near-blind woman who became lost and lay down to sleep. She awakened to find a huge elephant standing above her. Panic stricken, she remained motionless while the elephant and some companions covered her with branches and brush before leaving. She was rescued the next day when someone heard her cries for help.

Famed elephant researcher Cynthia Moss described unusual events in Tsavo National Park during the time when elephants were being poached by the Liangulu with poison-tipped arrows. The elephants didn't die immediately, and the hunters would wait sometimes for days before tracking the dying animal. When they found the corpse, rotting, they were able to pull out the tusks easily. But it had been observed that other elephants, discovering the carcass of their companion before the hunters, carried off tusks to hide them in the brush. Some tusks were found smashed against rocks.

A female, part of a family unit, tolerates a hitchhiking cattle egret on her back. Egrets feed on insects stirred up when elephants feed.

Such behavior is puzzling. For most animals, behavior is instinct-driven to serve some utilitarian purpose — food, survival from attack, mating, parental care. Elephants, however, have highly developed brains and store experiences in memory, like humans. Is it possible that some elephants have deduced that killing of their kin is for the tusks? In the case of elephants' interest in the bones of other elephants that died of natural causes, is it possible that their thought process allows them to speculate on death, like we do? Scientific researchers refuse to conjecture about such possibilities because it isn't possible to communicate with elephants to understand what they are thinking.

*   *   *

But elephants do communicate among themselves. When you watch a group of elephants, whether it is a family unit or a larger bond-group, you discover many subtle forms of communication. Elephants vocalize in different ways. The most common sound associated with them is trumpeting, a shrill blare made through their trunks. Not all trumpeting is the same, however. Elephant researchers Joyce Poole and Katherine Payne, in their years of painstaking research in Kenya's Amboseli National Park, have identified and interpreted several different kinds of trumpeting. For example, a pulsating trumpet signals that an individual is in a playful mood, while another, more nasal trumpet signifies a silly mood, sometimes followed by a nonsensical act such as picking up a tree branch and tossing it about. When an individual is surprised by something other than another elephant, it may emit a short, sharp trumpet signalling indignation. A long and shrill trumpet signifies social excitement, such as times when family units reunite with related kin.

Poole has identified fifteen varieties of an even more important form of communication: the rumble, often referred to as "stomach rumbles," though it has been determined that these sounds emanate from the larynx. These are low-frequency sounds, some of which are audible to humans, and some not. The tone and tenor of some rumbles can easily be mistaken for the roar of a distant lion. And, as with trumpeting, certain rumbles mean certain things. A long, soft rumble is a signal to move on, while a youngster may emit a short rumble that signifies that it is lost. Loud rumbles are used as a greeting for relatives. Finally, there is the contact call, a loud and long rumble that helps elephants determine location of family members when out of line of sight: "I'm over here, where are you?" "We're here."

Poole and Payne have discovered that elephants actually use infrasound, low-frequency rumbles below the level of human audibility, to communicate over very long distances. Low-frequency sound waves can travel over longer distances than high-frequency waves can because they are less affected by obstacles such as trees and land contours. In addition, these infrasound waves are often quite loud, with intensities of over one hundred decibels common. This means that elephants several miles apart are able to communicate with one another!

This discovery of long distance communication explains sometimes puzzling behavior of elephants that early researchers had observed, such as the nearly simultaneous arrival of different family units at the same water hole. One researcher in Zimbabwe, using radio-collared animals for tracking, had noted that family units separated by a couple of miles often moved in parallel grazing patterns; when one group changed direction, the other followed, even though they were well out of sight of each other.

Infrasound also plays an important role in mating. Because adult breeding males are not a part of family units and remain away from such groups most of the time, females coming into estrus need to announce their availability for mating. The results of their love calls are sometimes startling. Males are drawn from considerable distances, and when several arrive in close proximity simultaneously, there may be fighting — or at least intimidation by larger dominant males over smaller, younger ones. When mating has finished, the female often emits another low frequency rumble that brings her family unit to her, often with excited ear flapping and rumbles and trumpeting, as though in celebration.

*   *   *

Male elephants lead very different lives from females and the family units. As teenagers, the males are pushed out of family units to fend for themselves. Sometimes the males band together in temporary bachelor groups, but often they wander by themselves. But their wanderings keep them within communication distance of family units to which they are related and others.

Though they are sexually mature by their late

Some youngsters are bold, some shy. This one is expressing curiosity about our vehicle, raising its trunk to catch our scent.

teens, bulls do not begin to compete for breeding with females until their midtwenties. Dominance is established by age and size and through sparring, a semiplayful activity in which two males square off and engage tusks and trunks, pushing and shoving. This may go on over a period of time, with participants backing off, posturing, and reengaging. Though sparring rarely causes injury, it does help to establish which male is dominant.

By age thirty, bulls begin to experience a yearly period of intensified sexual and aggressive phenomenon known as musth. The length of time that a bull experiences musth is related to age. Bulls in their early thirties may stay in musth for a week or so. By their late forties, bulls may stay in musth for three months or more. Each male comes into musth at the same time each year.

During musth a fluid secretes from temporal glands behind the eyes, and there is a significant increase in aggression on the part of the bull due to elevated levels of testosterone. Poole has noted that a musth male also calls more frequently, using low rumbles, apparently trying to establish communication with females in estrus. And musth elevates the rank of dominance for bulls, making them more attractive to females. Even large nonmusth bulls will give way to a younger one in musth.

The level of aggressiveness gives rise to conflict that, on occasion, results in injury and even death of rivals. Such violent fights are rare, however. With their sophisticated means of long-distance communication, bulls in musth manage to avoid each other. When competing for a female in estrus, a musth male may choose to run off rather than fight with a challenger. However, if a battle does ensue, the tusks of the big bulls can become lethal weapons.

*   *   *

In addition to mutual protection and aid, the matriarchal family units serve another important function: a storehouse of knowledge. Because of their larger brains, elephants have good memories. Important information about food and water supplies during various seasons is remembered—and

Overleaf: A family unit heads toward its favorite water hole in late afternoon, grazing at leisure.

The mixed grasslands and savannah of Serengeti National Park in Tanzania. This vast park preserves habitat that has remained little changed for the past two million years.

Two elephants intertwine trunks and tusks in Kenya's Masai Mara National Reserve. Sometimes it's play, sometimes semiserious sparring, sometimes just expression of affection.

used. This knowledge is vital, for in times of drought it can mean survival for the family when normal water sources dry up. By moving to other places where the water may be more permanent and less affected by short dry periods, the family can survive.

Elephants also perpetuate traditions within family units. There are numerous instances where elephant families have been victims of poachers and hunters, and the older, surviving members have showed their offspring, by example, how to react violently or how to flee at the sight or smell of humans. This tradition can be passed on for several generations and accounts for the difference in behavior toward humans of different families in overlapping ranges. Some elephants have come to tolerate tourists in their domain, ignoring vehicles and jabbering people, while others, imprinted with the fear of hunters before there was a park or reserve, flee or behave with aggression.

In his studies at Lake Manyara in the 1960s, Iain Douglas-Hamilton noted such behavior on the part of certain elephant families. One unit, led by four large females, was particularly aggressive when it came to humans. Douglas-Hamilton speculates that this family had lived outside the park area in the 1950s in a place where newly settled Europeans were trying to create new farmland out of former elephant habitat. The humans declared war on the elephants, shooting some six hundred of them. Eventually this particular family found refuge in the newly established park, but they never lost their hatred of people. Douglas-Hamilton had two vehicles nearly demolished by this family, whereas other family units in the area remained docile in his presence.

In the early days of Eden, when our impact on the ecosystem was minimal, if nonexistent, elephants lived in a cyclic harmony with their environment. There were no artificial boundaries and no competition for land from bipeds. That delicate balance is now being tested.

These two males in Amboseli National Park engage in some semiserious sparring, usually conducted to establish dominance. Though violence is not common, some bulls in musth have engaged other males in battle over females, resulting in injury, sometimes death.

lock tusks . . .

They charge . . .

and back up.

In the Company of Elephants
A gallery of the African Elephant's Neighbors

Elephants have great impact on their environment. They prefer a habitat of mixed woodland and grassland, which gives them opportunity to eat a variety of vegetation. They are both browsers and grazers; they will eat rough sticks, stems and leaves of plants, as well as grasses and sedges and, when available, fruits. In the woodland areas of their habitat, elephants eat the bark and twigs and leaves of trees. Because of their size and strength, they are sometimes able to knock down trees to get at the green canopy normally out of reach. As a result, a too-large number of elephants in a given woodland area can kill most of the trees. This, in turn, opens up dense woodlands, converting the habitat to grasslands. The elephants then move on to another area of woodlands and the population of grazing animals in their previous habitat now increases.

As the grazers flourish in the new grasslands, they too begin to have impact. The antelope, gazelles, wildebeest, zebra, and others keep the grasses well cropped and, eventually, in certain areas the grass may become thin enough to allow seedlings of trees to take hold. Periodic fires that sweep grasslands kill seedling trees where grass is long and the fires burn hot. But if an area is cropped well by grazers, the young trees can take hold and grow. Soon they may be big enough to survive occasional light fires, and within a few decades a new forest is well on its way to flourishing. In most places in East Africa, this cy-

cle may take anywhere from seventy to one hundred years. By that time a new generation of elephants has converted other areas to grasslands and is ready to move back to the new forests.

Elephants are highly adaptable animals. The Great Namib Desert of Namibia, bordering on Africa's southwest coast, is an extremely arid place of blowing sands and fierce heat. Yet, despite these hostile conditions, several hundred elephants live here—have lived here for a long time, apparently. They've learned to migrate to places where they can dig for water and to find the meager vegetation to sustain themselves. This memory bank of knowledge has been the key to their survival. Should the matriarchs be killed, the younger ones would not know where to go to find life-giving water or forage.

In contrasting habitat, forest elephants live in dense rain forests of the central Congo River (Zaire River) Basin. Elephants occasionally venture into the treeless moorlands above 11,000 feet in the Aberdare Range in central Kenya. And before they became extinct, relatives of modern-day elephants, the mammoths, lived in subarctic climes, feeding on tundra plants in the frozen lands of Siberia and North America. The species is remarkably adaptable. Except when it comes to our technological killing power.

Zebras in Masai Mara National Reserve, Kenya.

Wild, or Cape hunting dogs in Serengeti National Park finish off a meal of Thomson's gazelle. They are one of East Africa's most endangered species; less than four hundred remain in the wild in Kenya.

A sleek and elegant Grant's gazelle in Tanzania's Ngorongoro Crater.

I arrived within moments after this pack of hyenas had taken down this zebra in Ngorongoro Crater. Within thirty minutes they had completely devoured it.

Gerenuks, sleek and graceful members of the gazelle family, often feed on leaves in this manner.

Two cheetahs on a hunt in Serengeti National Park, Tanzania pause to rest on a kopje *(literally, "island" of rock).*

Hippos gather in a pool in the Mara River, Masai Mara National Reserve, Kenya.

49

A leopard rests on a fallen tree at sunset in Samburu National Reserve in Kenya, preparatory to its evening hunt.

A Nile crocodile on the shore of Ewaso Nyiro in Samburu National Reserve in Kenya.

A lion snarls at my intrusion, guarding his wildebeest kill in Ngorongoro Crater.

Unless it has been rolling in mud, the black rhino is not black, but gray. One of Africa's most endangered species, it numbers less than four thousand across the continent. Ngorongoro Crater, Tanzania.

White rhinos are not native to Kenya, but are indigenous to nearby Uganda and many other parts of Africa. White rhinos are not white, but gray or whatever color the soil was in which they rolled last. The name is derived from Afrikaans, weit, *meaning "wide," because of their wide mouth, which is different from the more pointed mouth of the black rhino. Private game ranches in Kenya, such as Solio, have been successfully raising them in wild habitat and reintroducing these endangered animals to their former domain.*

Wildebeest gather for a crossing of the Mara River in Masai Mara National Reserve during the annual migration from Serengeti to the Mara. A lone elephant ignores the herd.

54

Tens of thousands of lesser flamingos feed in the shallow lake in Ngorongoro Crater.

Giraffe at sunset, Masai Mara National Reserve, Kenya.

This elephant in Tanzania's Lake Manyara National Park raises its trunk like an olfactory periscope to sniff the air for danger.

CRISIS IN EDEN

I had seen a herd of elephants travelling through dense native forest, pacing along as if they had an appointment at the end of the world. — Karen Blixen

*   *   *

About three million years ago, in the savannahs of East Africa, an interesting evolutionary experiment was underway. Descending from the trees inhabited by early apes came a new species, subsequently dubbed *Australopithecus africanus,* a small (average height about four feet) humanlike ape that walked erect. *A. africanus* was primarily a vegetarian, feeding on nuts, fruits, and berries found in abundance in the broad grasslands and savannahs. Though they walked upright, the members of this species had a decided apelike appearance, with flat noses and large brow ridges on the forehead. Their facial features were not unlike those of modern-day gorillas. They did not hunt elephants or any other species, though they may have, from time to time, scavenged dead game for meat. It's likely that these people held the elephant in awe, the giant of their domain. The elephants, in turn, accepted these innocuous bipeds as part of their realm, much like elephants today ignore the grazing animals around them.

Around two million years ago a new species gradually evolved from *Australopithecus*—*Homo habilis.* Of about the same height as its progenitor, the new species appeared to have a life-style similar to modern-day baboons—sleeping in trees at night, foraging over the ground during the day. There's evidence of use of tools made of animal bones and chipped stoned, but little to suggest use of weapons for hunting.

The next evolutionary succession was *Homo erec-*tus, with a significantly larger brain capacity and size than its predecessors. This species of early humans still retained some apelike features, but had smaller brow ridges and more humanlike stature (the average height was over five feet). *Homo erectus* made extensive use of tools, stone axes, chipped stones for skinning, and spears for hunting, and discovered the use of fire for warmth, protection, and cooking. Families made use of natural shelters such as caves and recesses. They were gatherers, nomadic, moving from place to place after a short stay in a given area, gathering fruits, nuts, berries, scavenged meat and occasional small mammals, all of which were brought back to camp to share communally. *Homo erectus,* however, had little impact on elephants and, like its predecessor, was probably accepted and integrated into the elephant's world.

Evolutionary momentum propelled *Homo erectus* toward *Homo sapiens* around five hundred thousand years ago. By that time, *H. erectus* had spread from Africa to Europe and across Asia. For a time, the two species coincided and, perhaps in isolated pockets, shared habitat. The newer species possessed greater intelligence, had a more intricate spoken language, and became an adept tool maker, rather than just a tool user. Instead of gatherer or forager, *H. sapiens* became a hunter-gatherer, using weapons to bring down bigger game. It's likely that these people banded together on occasion to hunt cooperatively, perhaps using fire to drive large animals over cliffs or into swamps where they could be killed more easily. It was a dangerous task, being armed only with spears. But being highly intelligent, the hunters could work together as a coordinated unit to surround their prey or lay an ambush.

A button worn by a park ranger at the entrance gate to Aberdare National Park in Kenya.

Signs in the window of Daphne Sheldrick's Animal Orphanage in Nairobi, Kenya.

An animal as large as an elephant could feed a large number of people, so the effort may have been justified. Perhaps, for the first time, the elephant began to fear its two-legged neighbor.

*   *   *

Until relatively recent times, hunters had less impact on elephants than farmers and builders of civilizations. Large and dangerous as an adversary, elephants could be killed with primitive weapons only under the best of conditions. As long as there was other, less dangerous game available, there was little reason to risk attacking so formidable an animal on any regular basis. And until about 1,500 years ago, there was no economic incentive.

Agriculture began about ten thousand years ago. At first it was rudimentary. Growth of certain plants was enhanced by crude irrigation to assure a supply. Later it was discovered that seeds could be planted to produce crops, but the crops required tending. Tending crops created the need to stay in a particular place. People congregated into villages

and then towns to be near their crops. As more people settled in a given area, they required more crops, resulting in larger areas that had to be used for growing. In time, as population and agriculture grew, the wildlife of certain areas was driven off so that crops could survive and sustain people. Domestication of animals for food came hand-in-hand with the development of agriculture and also competed with wild animals for habitat.

At the dawn of written history, about 3,500 years ago, the continent of Africa was populated with a rich diversity of cultures. In sub-Saharan Africa it was a population that was thinly scattered, clustered in various places with large areas unpopulated and still wild. Among the peoples were farmers, pastoralists, hunter-gatherers, hunters, and fishermen, all developed according to the suitability of the region in which they lived. In the forests of central Africa, people lived as hunter-gatherers. On the west coast, agriculture took hold and flourished. Later it spread, in pockets, across the continent to the east. In northern Africa, it was farming and herding of cattle, sheep, and camels.

Except in Egypt, where rich agricultural development created a highly developed civilization along the Nile, the human population of Africa remained relatively low, giving room for the wildlife. The human population was undoubtedly cyclic to some degree. In eras of good climate, plentiful food, and relative freedom from disease, the intelligent bipeds flourished, growing in number. At other times drought and famine, epidemics, natural calamities all served to keep *Homo sapiens* from becoming too populous. Like the populations of wildlife that shared our domain, humans came to a level of equilibrium with their environment. It was a balance that was not to last.

* * *

Our fascination with ivory may have begun with *Australopithecus,* or even earlier. Certainly by the time of evolution of *Homo,* this unusual substance was of interest. Finding the remains of a dead elephant would undoubtedly prompt investigation by hunter-gathers. Bones could serve some utility. Shattered, the sharp, splintered pieces could be used for digging or skinning or scraping. Later, when weapons were developed, they used the bone fragments as points for spears or arrows, although bone was brittle and broke easily. Ivory, too, could have been used in such utilitarian ways. But ivory was noticeably different from bone. It could be carved and shaped and polished. It took on forms that were beautiful. Moreover, it represented something unique about this awesome animal that shared our early world. Symbolically, power and strength were associated with the ivory from the huge elephants.

As early as forty thousand years ago, ivory figurines were made in Europe, at a time when our early ancestors shared habitat with wooly mammoths. When advanced civilizations developed in Egypt, the northern Mediterranean, China, India, and Arabia, ivory was a commodity of wealth, derived from trade. These trade networks developed in even the most remote areas, as long as there was some material gain for those involved, as there was particularly for manufactured items that were beyond the capability of local technology. Along the east coast of Africa, places such as Mombasa, Lamu, Pate, Zanzibar, Bagamoyo, and Pemba became important centers for exchange for traders from Egypt, the Middle and Far East, Arabia, and India. Later, Africa's west coast—the Ivory Coast—became a center for trade with Europe.

When such trade and commerce began over three thousand years ago, its impact on elephant population was negligible. Much of the ivory was probably gathered from carcasses of dead elephants. In the distant markets, ivory commanded a high price, and only the very wealthy could afford to buy the expensive carvings and ornaments. Demand probably remained moderate and could be satisfied largely with "found" ivory. But as successive civilizations flourished, demand for ivory increased.

The Greeks created lavish sculptures that were faced with ivory and overlaid with gold—so-called chryselephantine statues. In other places, monarchy prized ivory thrones—from India to Arabia, Turkey, Persia, and beyond. The Romans made the seats for their senate from the precious substance. In fact, during the zenith of the Roman Empire, ivory use was not limited to objects of art, but was used for such functional things as book covers, combs, hair ornaments, and even bird cages. Most of this ivory came from elephant populations in northern Africa and parts of Asia Minor. The North African population had been an isolated survivor of climatic change that widened the Sahara Desert, cutting off these elephants from the sub-Saharan stock. By the time of the close of the Roman empire, there were no more elephants in North Africa, and those of Asia Minor had probably disappeared.

Ivory remained in demand in Europe, but it became rare for a time. There were no easy trading routes across the Sahara from the interior of Africa where elephants were still plentiful. Eventually, the avenues of commerce were laid on the sea, and once again ivory trade flourished.

Between the seventh and eighth centuries, China was a major importer of ivory, obtained through Arab traders who, in turn, loaded their ships at such ports as Lamu and Zanzibar. It appears that the Chinese were as extravagant as the Romans in their use of ivory for decorative use. The tradition of creating intricate carvings in ivory, common in the Far East today, probably sprang from this era. By the Sung Dynasty (A.D. 960–1279) the Chinese had developed shipbuilding technology and opened trading routes that took their merchants from China to India where goods were exchanged: Chinese porcelain found its way by Indian merchants to East Africa and was traded for ivory and other goods.

The year 1497 marked another turning point in

As a sign that there has been little poaching here, this elephant family in Kenya's Amboseli National Park ignores people in vehicles.

African history, for it was the year that Portuguese explorer Vasco da Gama sailed around the Cape of Good Hope at the southern tip of Africa and began the era of European exploration and exploitation of the eastern coast of the continent. Prior to this, European merchants amassed their treasures from eastern Africa indirectly by forming ties with traders who brought goods overland, then across the Mediterranean, then overland again across southern Europe. Sailing ships could open direct trade with the heart of European countries. More important, Portugal was able to establish settlements on the eastern coast of the continent which, together with their settlements on Africa's west coast, provided a near monopoly on trade in gold, slaves, and ivory.

During the next three hundred years, other European countries established themselves in Africa. In West Africa, the French settled the area of the Senegal River, the British explored Gambia and the Gold Coast, and in southern Africa the Boers established settlements. The settlements by Europeans became

clustered along Africa's coasts where there was access to shipping by boats. "Darkest Africa," the vast and mysterious interior, remained unexplored by Europeans until the middle and late nineteenth century. There were several reasons for this—rivers that were not navigable because of rapids, hostile tribes, difficult terrain, and thick forest in many areas that made for difficult passage. But perhaps the major deterrent to exploration of the interior was a simple insect—the anopheles mosquito, bearer of the deadly disease malaria. Many early explorers, not aware that the disease was borne by mosquitos, died of "the fever."

Eventually, interior Africa was explored. In West Africa in the midnineteenth century, British, French, and Portuguese explorers and missionaries challenged the interior regions of the Congo River basin. A little later came the obsessive search on the part of British explorers to find the source of the Nile. The epic ventures of Speke and Burton led to the discovery of Lake Tanganyika and, eventually, of Lake Victoria as the source of the Nile. In south-central Africa, the Scottish missionary David Livingstone crossed the Kalahari Desert and explored the upper Zambesi River in what is now Zimbabwe, Zambia, and parts of Malawi. Later he moved northward toward Lake Tanganyika, where all communication with him was cut off for almost five years. His disappearance prompted the expedition in search of him, led by the American journalist Henry Morton Stanley. Stanley found Livingstone at Ujiji on the northeastern shore of Lake Tanganyika ("Dr. Livingstone, I presume?") in 1866.

The Stanley expedition marked a new era in African exploration. Not only was he well equipped and financed, but Stanley was able to fight off malaria by daily doses of a new drug, quinine. He returned to Africa for further exploration, transporting a steel-hulled boat overland to Lake Victoria where he sailed around. Later he did the same at Lake Tanganyika.

Stanley's explorations seemed to spark a renewed interest on the part of European nations in Africa. Soon, by the turn of the century, the continent was being carved up into various colonial empires. The vast region of the Congo came under the control of the King of Belgium — essentially a privately owned empire, until the Belgian government agreed to assume control. The French laid claim to Madagascar, which added to their already extensive holdings in West and North Africa. The Italians colonized Somalia and Eritrea. The Portuguese controlled Mozambique, Angola, and Portuguese Guinea. Tanganyika, parts of Cameroon, and Namibia came under the German empire. And the British empire controlled Sudan, Rhodesia, and Nyasaland (now Zimbabwe and Malawi), Bechuanaland (now Botswana), Uganda, and Kenya, along with smaller colonies. The map of Africa by the year 1900 looked like a gigantic jigsaw puzzle, made up of numerous European colonies.

*   *   *

One might assume that the major decline in elephant populations began with European colonization of Africa, but, in fact, there had been a long-established industry in ivory before the Europeans arrived. The demand for ivory from the Roman times onward had to be met, and found ivory, ivory obtained from already dead elephants, wasn't enough. When herds of elephants in North Africa were annihilated, sources for ivory had to be discovered elsewhere. Traders knew that the most

likely new supplies would come from Africa's east coast, probably the areas of Kenya and Tanzania, because they were both the highest density of elephants and within easy sailing distance of Arab and Indian traders. Places like Lamu, Pate, Mombasa, and Zanzibar were thriving seats of Swahili culture by the tenth century, a culture that was based on seagoing trade. Inland from these coastal cities, in the wilds of central Kenya and Tanzania, elephants were abundant.

There's good evidence that from the Middle Ages onward a well-developed and somewhat sophisticated commerce existed between interior tribal cultures and the coastal centers. The Liangulu, who were using their poison arrow technology in Tsavo as late as the 1940s, probably had a history of such hunting that goes back centuries. It's likely that the ancestors of modern-day Kamba people and the Dorobo, or Wandorobo, were part of this commercial network. Some hunted the elephant. Some gathered found ivory. Others specialized in transporting the goods to the coast. To all, ivory was a commodity that could be sold for the goods they coveted and needed — beads, cloth, shells, metal implements.

It's difficult to say how much impact on elephant population there was from this commerce. It's not likely to have been enough to cause a major decline. If the elephant populations were large to begin with, natural mortality would provide a large amount of found ivory. The hunters, even with their poison arrows and spears, were not as efficient at slaughter as modern hunters with modern weapons. Still, over the centuries there has been a decided downward trend in elephant populations across the continent, a decline that has accelerated rapidly in the last two hundred years. Elephants have always been smart enough to migrate to more secure places when threatened. The problem was, there were fewer and fewer safe places in which to hide.

*   *   *

By the end of the nineteenth century, when the trade in human slaves was also a conduit for ivory, there may have been several million elephants left on the African continent. Today, there are an estimated six hundred thousand — some think even less! Since midcentury, the slaughter of elephants has been enormous, and in the past two decades more than one million elephants have died. The two major causes have been increasing demand for ivory

Overleaf: A family unit gathers for an early morning drink at a favorite water hole in Amboseli National Park, Kenya. Such families consist of ten to twenty elephants, mostly females, calves, and young adults, led by an old matriarch who is the storehouse of knowledge.

Some youngsters are quite bold and will even charge vehicles as an act of bravado. Of course, it helps to have a five-ton momma backing you up.

and population pressure.

Africa has the fastest growing nations in the world. Twentieth-century medicine has changed rural Africa, but rural African culture has not changed significantly. In times past, famine and disease took its toll on families; two or three children might survive out of a dozen. Now they all survive, yet the ingrained cultural tradition of having large families remains. Kenya's growth rate is nearly 4 percent, compared to the world's average of 1.8 percent. As always, the elephant and other game are driven farther and farther back as the wave of humanity washes over the land.

Fortunately, starting early in this century, reserves and parks have been set aside, large, spacious areas where there is refuge from the onslaught of civilization. Most African nations have set aside significant land areas for such reserves. In some cases, the percent of total land area preserved exceeds that of the United States, long thought of as a leader in the conservation movement. Nearly 8 percent of Kenya's land area is preserved as national

parks or national reserves (game reserves). In Tanzania, that number is about 12 percent of total land area. Even tiny Rwanda has set aside nearly 20 percent of its land area as forest reserve or parks, though there are almost no elephants left in that country. The preserved land areas mean nothing, however, as long as there is great demand for ivory, and poachers are willing to risk their lives for the profit.

The demand for ivory and ivory products can be attributed directly to increased affluence in developed nations where unthinking buyers purchase things ranging from mere trinkets to expensive carvings. Artisans in the Far East, drawing on centuries of skill, mass produce these items for export to the United States or European countries or for sale in local tourist shops. Undeniably, there's beauty in certain ivory carvings. Yet the buyer rarely associates a carving or trinket in a showcase with a dead elephant.

However, there are hopeful signs of change. The widespread publicity associated with the elephant

Harmon is one of Cynthia Moss's study elephants in Amboseli National Park. The scar on his left leg is from a wire snare used by meat poachers outside the park. Harmon had to be tranquilized and the wound treated to prevent infection.

crisis has caused a marked reduction in purchase of ivory products and a reduced demand for ivory. Continued public awareness of the issue will help immeasurably. And it is hoped that a continuation of the ban on ivory imports in the United States and other major countries will keep the price of ivory low enough to minimize poaching.

Alleviating population pressures will take longer. Old traditions and cultural inheritances change slowly. Oria Douglas-Hamilton, who, along with her husband Iain, is considered one of the world's experts on elephants, expresses optimism from her home in Kenya. "Attitudes are changing. There is more emphasis now on family planning and I'm confident that people will change."

In my numerous trips to East Africa, my guide and driver for most of my safaris has been John Lidede, a native Kenyan and a superb game spotter. Over the years, Lidede (he prefers that to "John") and I have become good friends. We call each other *ndugu* (brother), and we talk extensively about problems in Africa and elsewhere. Lidede has eight children, and it has been a great struggle for him to feed and clothe and educate his family, but he has done it. "When our country became independent, our President Kenyatta told us to have many children and that life would be good for us. But now we know that there are problems with too many people. So I tell my children that they must have only two children. And things will be better for us."

THE POLITICS
OF IVORY

It begins in a dismal little shop on a back street of Hong Kong, a place where the air is filled with chalky white dust of ivory. The whine of high-speed drills permeates a room where some workers, the more skilled, carve the white gold into intricate designs, creating works of art, while others produce simple objects like rings or beads to be strung into necklaces. One of the larger families in the ivory business boasts that it can produce up to one hundred thousand rings or forty thousand necklaces a month. All these items, from expensive carvings to cheap trinkets, will end up in shops throughout the Far East—in Singapore, Kuala Lumpur, Tokyo, Bangkok, and other cities large and small that attract tourists.

The workers sit amid stacks of tusks, most of them illegally obtained. As much as 80 percent of such ivory comes from poaching. All of it has cost the lives of thousands of elephants, but the workers here have no real knowledge of the origin of their livelihood. Many of these craftsmen are descended from a long lineage of ivory carvers and, given the chance, their progeny would continue the tradition. Some of them believe that elephants shed their tusks. Most really don't care about the fate of elephants.

The merchants who own these businesses talk of ivory purchases not by the pound, but by the ton. How much is a ton of ivory? In 1979 when 520 tons of ivory were shipped to Hong Kong, it represented the deaths of thirty-one thousand elephants—or about sixty elephants to the ton. By 1988, 290 tons came from the killing of thirty-three thousand elephants, or about 114 elephants to the ton. The difference comes from the fact that, in recent years,

the average size of tusks from poached elephants has diminished greatly. Many of the older, larger-tusked animals have been killed off. And as long as the price of ivory remains high, the numbers of elephants slaughtered increases to keep pace with demand.

Until recently, ivory played an important role in the economy of the Far East and in other sectors of the world. The number of people who earned their living as traders, carvers, and merchants numbered in the tens of thousands. Some estimates ran as high as fifty thousand, with about thirty thousand of those in Japan alone. The annual revenue worldwide from the ivory industry in the late 1980s was estimated at between $500 million and $1 billion a year, creating a strong economic incentive for illicit trade in ivory.

In the mid-1970s, one hundred nations worldwide agreed to become a part of the Convention on International Trade in Endangered Species (CITES), the treaty to regulate trade in ivory and other products of threatened animals. With many species being threatened with extinction because of the increased value of fur, hide, and tusks, the creation of CITES was an important first step in preventing such extinction. With an office in Lausanne, Switzerland, CITES established an ivory unit, with an annual operating budget of over $350,000, to deal with the sticky business of regulating the ivory trade.

Under regulations adopted in 1986, CITES required nations producing ivory to establish export quotas that would ensure the safety of existing elephant populations. The system required that each tusk be marked with a unique serial number to be

In some East African parks and reserves, large-tusked elephants have become rare because of past poaching. This old bull has survived in the good protection of Ngorongoro Crater in Tanzania.

computerized for tracking and inventory purposes. The scheme was designed to provide CITES and member nations the means to track the flow of ivory from producing countries to consumer countries. Unregistered ivory would be considered illegal, and it was assumed that consumer countries would bar the import of unregistered tusks. Unfortunately, the system didn't work. One reason was that the exporting countries established their own quotas, and they required no scientific confirmation of the levels of the quotas. Another reason: In anticipation of the regulations, some ivory traders in Hong Kong and Singapore imported many tons of tusks before the October 31, 1986, deadline. Even worse, the next few years saw many abuses of the CITES regulation—falsified export documents, ignored quotas, bribed officials. In Burundi, where elephants no longer existed, ninety tons of ivory were registered for export to the Far East. Obviously such ivory was obtained from poaching, probably in Kenya and Tanzania, then smuggled into Burundi—often in the false bottoms of fuel tanker trucks. CITES attempted to strike a bargain with Burundi officials, offering to register the obviously illicit ivory if it would get out of the trade. But one CITES official admitted that "we got snookered." Burundi continued in the business, acquiring another ninety tons or more of poached ivory to sell.

The CITES ivory unit itself came under fire from conservationists, who suggested that it was too willing to accommodate the ivory traders, rather than taking a hard-nosed attitude on illicit ivory trade. Indeed, nearly two-thirds of the ivory unit's budget was from contributions by ivory traders. One CITES regulatory official resigned when he learned that his salary was being paid by the very traders he was trying to regulate.

When poaching reached its zenith in 1988, the economic incentive for illicit trade created an intricate network of ivory movement worldwide. Unlike drugs, which can be smuggled in small quantities, tusks, to retain their value, must be shipped intact. One would think that their very size and bulk would make for difficult shipment surreptitiously, yet ingenious methods were devised. Like drugs, there were quick, huge profits to be made. And, as in the drug trade, the profits tempted some government officials into corrupt practices. A member of Tanzania's parliament was sentenced to a twelve-year prison sentence for possessing 105 tusks that were obviously aimed for sale on the illegal market.

Foreign embassy officials have been caught trying to smuggle ivory; one was found with more than two hundred tusks worth an estimated $1.5 million.

*   *   *

Once a tusk is hacked out of the still-warm body of a slain elephant, it takes a devious path to find its way into the hands of ivory merchants and traders. The ivory trail in Africa has varied in recent years, depending on the latest regulations and the newest loopholes. The payloads of ivory seem to follow the laws of thermodynamics, flowing over the path of least resistance and maximum corruption. Some African countries seem to have little concern about the poaching crisis. Other countries such as South Africa, Botswana, and Zimbabwe continue to actively promote international trade in ivory.

Typical of the rationale of the three countries, Zimbabwe officials claim that they have a "surplus" of elephants that need to be "cropped" (meaning slaughtered) periodically to maintain a balance. The sale of this cropped ivory provides funds for carrying out conservation programs, it is claimed. The cropping is done in two ways: by game management teams and by hunting. For a mere $30,000 or so, a game hunter equipped with the latest high-powered rifle can live out a Hemingway-esque fantasy by blasting an elephant. Game officials, working in teams, periodically shoot whole families of elephants to "control" populations in the game parks and, thus, balance the animals to the resource. In both cases, tusks are sold on the world market for a good profit and the funds are used for further game management. This good management, it is claimed, is why Zimbabwe's elephant population has been increasing and is free of poaching.

The clarity of this logic, however, is distorted by smoke and mirrors. Ivory profits by this scheme have been used to create artificial game environments, usually by drilling new water wells, as at Hwange National Park in Zimbabwe. These artificial water holes enable a greater density of elephants to survive in the region than would normally adapt to this dry environment. With increased population comes a "need" to crop, with its attendant profit from ivory sale. The scheme seems more directed toward ivory profits—an ivory factory mentality—than good biological management.

There's a subtle but important distinction to be made between game management and habitat management philosophies. In the former, manage-

Are ivory knickknacks really worth it? (Photo © by Gordon Maltby)

A collection of confiscated tusks in a warehouse in Kenya's Tsavo National Park. Fortunately, the worldwide ivory ban and resultant plunge in ivory prices has greatly diminished poaching in the past year.

ment schemes are directed toward manipulating habitat to promote certain species, as in the case of Zimbabwe developing artificial water holes to increase elephant populations. When habitat is manipulated to promote dominance of certain species—to enhance tourism or hunting, for example—other species may suffer. These other species are often the lesser known, less spectacular animals, but they are important, nonetheless, as part of a complex ecosystem. The manipulation of game may lead, ultimately, to biological impoverishment of certain regions by skewing the biological diversity in favor of one or two species. The imbalance often creates conditions in which further manipulation is required, the killing of elephants, for example, because there are too many for the limited resource of the environment.

In the philosophy of habitat management, the ideal situation is one in which an entire ecosystem is preserved and allowed to maintain itself, through the constant change and cycles of ecosystem dynamics. It takes into account predator-prey relationships and the cycles where certain species may experience population growth, then decline as disease and/or habitat change cause rapid die-off. The ideal is a park or reserve large enough to allow for movement and migration, unhindered, and for changes to take place in certain parts of the habitat while other parts may be recovering. For example, elephants change their habitat by destroying, over time, the woodlands. When these are gone, they move on to other mixed woodland areas. The former habitat goes through a slow transition to grassland and then, later, back to woodland. The time required for this transition may be a century or more, and the habitat must be large enough to support the elephants in other woodland areas while the first is recovering.

Unfortunately, this ideal situation is rarely achieved. Most national parks and game reserves are far too small to allow such natural cycles. Moreover, it's often political rather than ecological considerations that determine the boundaries of the protected area. It's often necessary to strike a com-

Another place where poaching has been severely limited, resulting in survival of big tuskers, is Kenya's Amboseli National Park. The high density of tourism discourages poaching activity because of the high risk of detection.

promise between protected reserves and land to be used for human development. In African nations, in particular, this compromise is necessary because of burgeoning population. To their credit, such countries as Kenya and Tanzania have preserved a higher percentage of their land area as game reserves and parks than many developed nations around the world. In Kenya, about 8 percent of its land area is preserved, while in Tanzania the figure is nearly 12 percent.

The reality of game or habitat management in African nations is one of economics in most cases. In the case of Zimbabwe, game management is used to promote a surplus of elephants for hunting and cropping, with income being derived from sale of ivory. Elephants must be killed to produce income. In East Africa—Kenya and Tanzania—habitat management preserves ecosystems, more or less, and big game hunting is banned in Kenya. Income is derived by tourists who come here to view the wildlife and the wildlife habitat in an unspoiled, unmanipulated state. Species such as elephants need not be killed to provide income. In fact, Richard Leakey, director of Kenya Wildlife Service, points out that in peak years Kenya tourism brings in roughly $400 million in income, which, divided by Kenya's twenty thousand remaining elephants, means that each elephant is worth approximately $20,000 per year in tourist income—far more than would result from killing it and selling the ivory.

*　　*　　*

By 1989 poaching in East Africa had reached crisis proportions. Countries such as Kenya were likely to have no elephants left in a few years unless something drastic was done. The situation was compounded by the deaths of some tourists, including one American, at the hands of poachers who had turned to freelance banditry. Kenya could ill afford to lose its tourist income (second only to coffee export as a foreign currency producer), and that seemed likely as news of elephant and rhino slaughter and tourist deaths made world headlines.

In April 1989, Kenya's president, Daniel arap Moi, announced the appointment of Richard Leakey as head of the Kenya Wildlife Service. Leakey, then 44, and the son of famed anthropologists Louis and Mary Leakey, learned of his appointment one morning on a Nairobi news broadcast as he was heading to work as director of Kenya's National Museum. A quick phone call to the presi-dent's office confirmed the news report.

With his usual energy, Leakey immediately set about changing the organization that had become lax, inert, corrupt, and ineffective over the years into a "parastatal," that is, a semiautonomous entity free of political appointments and influence. A transfusion of new people into the organization began to have immediate effect. By overcoming the Kenya Wildlife Service's image of being an ineffective agency, Leakey was able to successfully solicit donations from various countries and organizations of badly needed equipment. These supplies ranged from vehicles and aircraft to modern weapons to be used by antipoaching rangers. There was also money to pay rangers a decent enough salary to take away incentive for corrupt practices.

At Leakey's urging, President Moi agreed to demonstrate to the world Kenya's commitment to saving the elephant. In July of 1989, he set ablaze a mountain of confiscated tusks, about three thousand of them worth an estimated $3 million. Though sale of the tusks might have provided further funding for antipoaching efforts, such sales could be likened to the U.S. Drug Enforcement Agency selling cocaine and heroin to support its activities.

In his first year on the job, Leakey could point to spectacular results: armed poachers shot, scores arrested, increased patrolling by more skilled and better equipped rangers, and a rate of slaughter of elephants that dropped from a thousand or more per year in Tsavo alone to less than a hundred.

Other important forces were at work in 1989, fueled by growing public outrage at elephant slaughter. In June the United States declared a moratorium on the commercial import of ivory. The European Economic Community followed suit a few days later. In October, CITES met in Lausanne, Switzerland, and the member nations voted to ban international trade in ivory and other elephant products. Even Japan, a big player in the ivory game, submitted to the ban. China did not, but with other nations halting imports, the market for China's ivory appeared to be drying up. Three other member nations refused to honor the ban: South Africa, Zimbabwe, and Botswana, again arguing that their game management policies promoted "surplus" elephant populations that need periodic cropping.

The effect of the ban has been phenomenal. By mid-1990 the price of ivory that once averaged be-

Overleaf: A lone male grazes placidly in Kenya's Masai Mara National Reserve. Some elephants have migrated here to Masai Mara from nearby Serengeti National Park in Tanzania because of greater poaching activity.

tween $200 and $300 a kilogram had dropped to as low as $2 in East Africa and as little as $20 a kilo in Central Africa. Together with a tougher antipoaching program, the ban has made it, in the words of Richard Leakey, "not worth the effort or risk to kill elephants at the present value of ivory. There is no future in ivory trading."

Perhaps. But there is evidence that pressure is mounting to replace the ban with regulated ivory trade at the next CITES meeting in 1992. Back to business as usual. The exporters of southern Africa will have the support of the ivory traders of the Far East, and countries like Zimbabwe continue to argue that ivory trade is vital to the maintenance of its conservation program.

Southern African wildlife experts estimate that it costs a minimum of $200 per square kilometer of land area to effectively protect elephants and other wildlife against poaching. (In other countries, however, the cost per acre is much lower.) Officials in Zimbabwe and other countries argue that sale of ivory is needed to pay that high cost. A continued ivory ban will keep the price of ivory low, making the risk-to-profit ratio far too high for poachers. Thus, the cost of protecting against poaching will be lower, and properly developed tourism can pay for much of that.

And besides, do we really need ivory trinkets?

*　　*　　*

In April of 1989 I walked into a shop in Kuala Lumpur, Malaysia's modern, bustling capital. It was a shop specializing in crafts, and I asked the shopkeeper about the ivory carvings. Were they made from legally obtained ivory? He seemed somewhat offended at my query. Of course it was all legal. Were there documents? Well, the carvers had proper documents to prove legality, but once the ivory was carved, there was no need. Of course. What will happen, I asked, when there are no more elephants? Not to worry, he said. Everything is now carefully regulated and controlled to protect elephants. In his mind he wasn't lying. He believed what he said. But I knew better.

Like human youngsters, an elephant calf can be a nuisance to siblings. Here, a youngster climbs on a sleeping sister or brother in Kenya's Masai Mara National Reserve. (Photo © by Edward Borg.)

74

TANZANIA

The landscape of Tarangire National Park in the northeast part of Tanzania is right out of the Jurassic Age. It could well have served as model for one of those paintings in *National Geographic* magazine depicting the age of dinosaurs. You expect, at any moment, to see a *Stegosaurus* or *Triceratops* or perhaps even a *Tyrannosaurus rex* wandering amid those eerily prehistoric baobab trees. It is thick with giant baobab trees, probably the greatest concentration of them left in East Africa. And there are expansive grasslands, graceful acacias, and doum palms that rise tall on slender trunks to branch into several arcs of fluttering palm leaves. However, it is the *mbuyu*, or baobab, that dominates this land.

The baobab is the tree of life and the tree of mystery and legend. It is said, backed by some scientific evidence, to be among the oldest of living things, more than two thousand years old in some cases. It is, according to African lore, the tree where man was born. With squat trunk and stubby branches, it looks like a tree that has been uprooted and stuck back into the ground upside down. But it is elegant in both form and function; there is a stark, primal beauty to the baobab, and it is useful to both humans and animals. The nuts are a source of food, requiring only to be pounded a little on stone and then cooked on a slow fire. The tree provides welcome shade for animals and nesting for numerous birds. Sometimes those fat trunks develop hollows, to which elephants contribute when they strip away bark and gouge the trunks with their tusks. These hollows, cool, shaded, and protected, often hold water from previous rains long after moisture has evaporated from surrounding land. And they are often sites for bee hives, again providing sustenance for both humans and animals.

In one place in Tarangire I found a huge baobab whose center was completely hollowed out, possibly by elephants. It brought to mind fairy tales, where gnomes might live in such a place, or Tolkien and his Hobbits. The diameter of the trunk was about fifteen feet, and the hollow interior extended about twelve feet above the base. It made a snug and waterproof hideaway for anyone passing by, and charcoal on the dirt floor was evidence that it had, in fact, been used by people—perhaps honey hunters.

It was in Tarangire where I found the largest herd of elephants I had ever seen. When I first spotted them, they were gray specks off in the distant wash of yellow grasses to the north of the track. But they were moving slowly in our direction, and it seemed worthwhile to wait until they came closer. A rough count made them out to be at least 150 in number, maybe 175. Maybe more. It was far bigger than the big groups of Kenya's Amboseli National Park.

While waiting for the elephant herd to come closer, I looked out over this landscape of Tarangire, admiring the vastness of it all. And at that moment I felt a stab of intense pain on my left arm, like the jab of the point of a sharp knife. Something had bitten me! I swatted, but the insect was elusive and flew off unharmed. A tsetse fly. I've been nailed by blackflies in Alaska, deerflies in Utah, and horseflies in numerous places, but with a mouth like a mini-chain saw, the tsetse is infinitely more painful and persistent than anything we have in North America. Curiously, however, these obnoxious little critters have had great and beneficial impact on game by limiting or even preventing the spread of human activities throughout much of sub-Saharan Africa.

An insect of brush country, the tsetse sucks the

Ngorongoro Crater Conservation Area in Tanzania lies east of Olduvai Gorge and Serengeti National Park. It's considered part of the Serengeti ecosystem. The high walls of the crater form a barrier to protect against poaching.

blood of warm-blooded animals, including humans. It is also the vector for trypanosomiasis, known by its more unpleasant name of "sleeping sickness," which kills cattle and, sometimes, people. Over eons the native herbivores of Africa have developed an immunity to trypanosomiasis, but cattle have no such immunity. Where the tsetse flourishes, settlers and their cattle do not, thus sparing the habitat of indigenous animals from being turned into grazing land.

Nursing my wound, and keeping a sharp eye out for any more tsetses, I watched as the elephant herd moved closer and individual animals began to loom large before us. They knew we were here—our group was in two separate Land Rovers parked close together—but it didn't deflect the animals at all from their intended path—straight in our direction. On the opposite side of the dirt road on which we were parked there was more grassland, and then the land dipped away to the broad valley of the Tarangire River, the only permanent water in this region. The river was their obvious destination.

As the first front of them drew closer, the animals hesitated before proceeding. The rear guard lumbered forward and caught up to the stationary front, pressuring the leaders to move onward. Like a wave parting around a rock, they began to separate and the herd flowed around our vehicles, keeping a reasonable distance—reasonable, I suppose, for elephants, but somewhat too close for me. In a few moments I suddenly realized that we were completely surrounded by elephants. They blocked our track in front and back. But they moved slowly, with no apparent sign of being agitated by the presence of people in their midst. It seemed as though it was to be a passive encounter. However, one obnoxious, prepubescent youngster caught our scent and decided to become macho. With blaring, trumpeting charges, this teenage punk challenged our vehicles. Backing off, he grabbed trunkfuls of grass and threw them into the air, dirt clumps and all. Some of the detritus showered down on his head and seemed to make him even angrier. He charged again, head up, ears at full flap, and blaring out a defiant challenge.

The act was repeated several times. It was comical, but I wasn't laughing at the moment. They were bluff charges, never more than a hundred feet in approach, but I was concerned that the other elephants would become alarmed. Being totally surrounded by a herd of elephants was one thing, but being sur-

A herd of elephants, numbering almost two hundred, in Tanzania's Tarangire National Park. Such large herds are made up of several related family units and are usually temporary aggregations.

rounded by a herd of *angry* elephants was something I did not care to hazard.

Hussein Hamisi, my guide, laughed at the antics. "Aren't you afraid the herd will charge?" I asked. "*Hakuna wasi-wasi*," he replied. ("There is no worry.") "He is trying to be a big shot, but the *mzees* [wise elders] know better."

Hussein was right. The elders remained wise and calm and the group slowly moved on, heading for the waters of the Tarangire River in fading twilight. The young protagonist went with them, shaking his head, flapping those gargantuan ears, and waving his trunk in bravado. (*Guess I showed those bipeds a thing or two.*) The rest of the herd ignored the upstart.

That encounter occurred in 1988. A year later my experience was totally different.

*   *   *

When I returned to Tarangire in 1989 it was about the same time of year. Judging from the condition of the grasslands it appeared that there had been a normal amount of rainfall. And herds of grazing animals seemed to be about the same in number. But there were very few elephants. Moreover, the elephants we did see acted very nervous. Several small groups fled at the sound and sight of vehicles, crashing off through the brush in clouds of dust. A group of five males of differing ages didn't flee, but they nervously tested the air with upraised trunks when our vehicle stopped for photographs. In two days of driving through the park we saw no signs of that enormous herd of the previous year.

I was dismayed. My initial conclusion was that there had been a marked increase in poaching in the region. Although that may have been true, there are some other plausible explanations as well. Large herds such as the one I saw in 1988 are temporary groupings. Eventually, the different family units break off and go their own ways.

Still, I was concerned about a possible stepped-up killing of elephants in the region. Park officials could not confirm that there had been a significant increase in poaching activities, and so the sparsity of elephants remained a mystery.

*   *   *

In 1990 the elephant situation seemed even worse in Tarangire. Over a two-day period I drove most of the road system in the park, covering much of Tarangire's total area, and saw six elephants. Admittedly, elephants do move around over large areas, and the family units, separately or as herds, could range outside the park. But much of the land adjacent to Tarangire is divided up into *shambas,* or farms. And outside the park elephants would be more exposed to poachers, forcing them to return to the sanctuary of the national park.

When I met with David Babu, Tanzania's director of national parks, he was frank about his country's poaching problems and the declining elephant populations. "Only three or four years ago there were perhaps four thousand elephants in Serengeti. Now there are only about four hundred and fifty." (An important point here: these figures do not necessarily suggest that all those elephants have been killed. There is evidence that, with increasing poaching pressure in Serengeti, many elephants have migrated northward into Kenya's Masai Mara Game Reserve where antipoaching efforts are much better and elephants are more secure.)

Babu's figures for other parks and reserves were equally distressing. The famous Selous reserve in southern Tanzania, and the largest in that country at twenty-one thousand square miles in area, had an estimated one hundred thousand elephants in the 1970s. Today there are only thirty thousand—possibly less—according to game census figures. At Lake Manyara National Park, a small but significant reserve west of Tarangire and site of Iain Douglas-Hamilton's famous studies, there were 450 elephants four to five years ago. Today, 150.

Curiously, when I asked Babu about Tarangire's elephants, his figures seemed to indicate that the population was stable. A 1980 census estimated about three thousand elephants for the greater Tarangire ecosystem, which includes areas outside the park. However, when I met with Tarangire's senior park warden, Isaac Muro, he insisted that the park's elephants have actually *increased* in population by a significant amount. According to Muro, a 1987 census showed five thousand elephants living in the Tarangire ecosystem, and by 1990 there were an estimated 6,200.

Where were they? I recounted my observations of 1988, 1989, and 1990 to both men, asking if this might not be evidence of declining elephant numbers. But they suggested that during the latter two years some of the elephants may have temporarily moved to areas outside the park. Maybe. But I was still skeptical.

My conversation with Muro was enlightening in other ways. I had a chance to observe some of the

An old male in Tanzania's Ngorongoro Crater Conservation Area. Males tend to inhabit the crater floor, while females in family units inhabit the forests of the crater rim.

A young male, left, probably just off on its own from a family group, roams the yellow-barked acacia forest with an old bull in the floor of Ngorongoro Crater.

park's forty-five-member antipoaching force, in this case a pitifully equipped handful of men. Of the five men, two had uniforms. One wore badly worn patent leather loafers instead of combat boots. Rifles were World War I vintage of different calibers. But that didn't matter, for they admitted that they didn't have any ammunition just then anyway. If the poachers in Tanzania are armed with AK-47 or G-3 automatic weapons, as are the *shifta* in Kenya, these guys don't stand a chance.

Muro was frank about the inadequate funding for antipoaching activities in Tanzania. Low salaries make it difficult to recruit good men. A starting ranger here earns 3,040 Tanzania shillings a month, which translates to $16 a month! Out of that must come taxes (about one hundred shillings a month for a single person), food, and lodging. One beer at the nearby Tarangire Safari Lodge would cost a person ten percent of the monthly salary. If the ranger were trying to build a home for his family, a single bag of cement costs 1,200 shillings and one piece of roofing sheet is 2,200 shillings. Such meager wages

hardly inspire careers in wildlife conservation. In fact, it's hard to blame the rangers if they accept a little *chai* (literally "tea," meaning bribe money) from poachers. Survival takes precedence over altruism.

Muro himself is fiercely dedicated to protecting Tarangire and its wildlife. He speaks with love about this place and even plants young baobab trees in protected plots (many young trees are destroyed by periodic fires). Yet, even with a college education and a degree in wildlife management, he earns 7,020 shillings a month, equivalent to $37 a month.

When I left Tarangire, it was with a feeling of profound sadness, bordering on depression. Several months later, after I had returned to Colorado, I met a woman at a party who had just returned from Tanzania. She talked excitedly about her adventures. The highlight of her trip, she said, had been an encounter with a huge herd of elephants, possibly two hundred or more, in Tarangire National Park!

*   *   *

Northwest of Tarangire is Lake Manyara—

Tarangire National Park, Tanzania, is one of East Africa's loveliest settings, with its grasslands and forests of ancient baobab trees. Some baobabs may be two thousand years old or older.

Hemingway country. In *The Green Hills of Africa,* the author describes his hunting safari in the regions east and north of this lake which sits at the base of the western escarpment of the Rift Valley.

It was a green, pleasant country with hills below the forest that grew thick on the side of a mountain, and it was cut by the valleys of several watercourses that came down out of the thick timber on the mountain. . . . If you looked away from the forest and the mountain side you could follow the watercourses and the hilly slope of the land down until the land flattened and the grass was brown and burned and, away, across a long sweep of country, was the brown Rift Valley and the shine of Lake Manyara.

From Tarangire you can drive west to Kwa Kuahinia and the new Arusha-to-Dodoma Highway that seems perennially under construction, then north to Makuyuni, then west on the incredibly dusty road that leads to Mto Wa Mbu, one of my favorite villages in East Africa (the Swahili name means River of Mosquitoes). Here it's a mandatory

stop to buy a not-so-cold beer from a little *duka* on the main street, necessary to wash down the dust in your throat, and to visit the stalls of the craftsmen selling carvings and Masai spears and trinkets to the increasing numbers of tourists passing through. The greying woodcarver, whose tin-covered stall is way in the back, is a nearly blind old *mzee,* but his ebony wood carvings are still the best. From Mto Wa Mbu, it's a short distance to the entrance to Lake Manyara National Park.

On previous trips to Manyara this is the route I normally took. But in February of 1990, I came into the park the back way, from the south, on a route rarely used by tourists. From Tarangire we headed south to the village of Mbuyu wa Germanie, "The Baobab of the Germans," a former outpost of German soldiers in World War I. Following the mandate of the mother country in Europe, the German colony of Tanganyika, later to become Tanzania, was at war with British colonial Kenya. In 1917 this encampment probably bristled with wartime activity, for the Kenya border lay to the north only

83

A nervous male tests the air in Tarangire National Park, Tanzania. Such nervousness is often caused by poaching activity in the region.

120 miles away. In 1990, however, any traces of an outpost were long since gone, and there was no longer a baobab tree to mark its location. From the sleepy little collection of huts and houses, we headed west toward the imposing escarpment forming the western wall of the Rift Valley. The road wound through flat savannah country with lovely grassy swales and thornbush acacias. At a place called Mbugwe sits an abandoned mission/church built in 1916. Weeds and grass grew up tall in the old cemetery. The mission itself echoed of a past attempt to settle the region; undoubtedly, European farmers tried to till the lands nearby, fighting off the grazing herds of wildebeest and the elephants to protect their crops. There were few signs left of farms. Only as we approached the south boundary of Lake Manyara National Park did we see evidence of contemporary agriculture.

Lake Manyara is a soda lake with no outlet, formed by waters draining the plateau above the escarpment and plunging down as numerous streams to feed the lake. In addition, the fractured volcanic rock forming the wall of the escarpment has countless subterranean pathways for seeping groundwater to work its way to the base, providing another source for Manyara's waters.

Lake Manyara National Park is not large—only 123 square miles in area—but at one time it had the highest density of elephants of any place in Africa. This was in the late 1960s and early 1970s when Iain Douglas-Hamilton conducted his famous studies of Manyara's elephants, described in his fine book, with wife Oria, *Among the Elephants.*

Why was Manyara's elephant density so high? Some of it seemed related to human population pressure in lands surrounding the park, driving more elephants from former habitat into the relative security of the park. The park itself has an unusual habitat, consisting primarily of groundwater forest in the northern half and mixed acacia woodland in the south. The groundwater forest is particularly thick and lush, resembling a tropical rain forest. It is not rain, however, that is responsible for this rich verdancy. The high water table, created by seepage from the adjacent escarpment, provides all the necessary moisture for this fecundity. As you drive through it, there's a distinct feeling of being transported to a scene in one of those *Tarzan* jungle movies. Any moment you expect to see Johnny Wiesmuller swing out of a tree on one of the many vines.

With this rich vegetative environment, the

Part of a large herd of elephants in Tanzania's Tarangire National Park. Made up of numerous family groups, such herds travel and feed together for a period of time then break up into their respective family units again.

elephants here have plenty to eat. However, in 1971, when Iain Douglas-Hamilton was concluding his studies, the population was well over five hundred in the park and Iain was fearful that the mature *Acacia tortilis* trees — a particularly favored food of the elephants — would all be killed by the elephants within ten years. Iain was concerned that culling of elephants by shooting might be necessary to preserve the remaining habitat. Nothing was ever done and eventually the problem took care of itself. Within a few years the elephant population declined by about one hundred animals. More significantly, however, later studies showed that remaining elephants had reduced their feeding on the acacias. New growth took hold and today there are still thick acacia forests alongside the groundwater forest.

The elephant population of Lake Manyara National Park has diminished from about 450 in 1977 to 150 today. Undoubtedly poaching has taken its toll here, particularly among those animals that have strayed outside the park boundaries. Those re-

maining seem placid enough in the presence of people, indicating, perhaps, that poaching pressure has eased off.

I eased into the park at the south entrance, at the Iyambe Ranger Post, which, for lack of tourists who come this way, was deserted. The road is rough, requiring four-wheel drive, which probably accounts for the lack of visitors to this part of the park. The forest here is thick, comprised mostly of big, yellow-barked acacias, and it was into one of these groves that we pulled to visit the Maji Moto Camp of Alfredo Pelizzoli. A former big game hunter, Alfredo is building a new tented lodge under permit from the Tanzania parks system. When completed it will offer visitors a splendid sense of isolation in this wild part of Manyara. Nearby is a lovely thermal spring, *Maji Moto* (Hot Water), that bubbles from the basaltic rock at the base of the escarpment. A short walk from the camp is the southern shore of the lake, curtained by marshes, with flights of flamingos silhouetted each dawn against the rising sun. Not far away elephants trumpeted.

Photographers in Tarangire National Park, Tanzania, enjoy the spectacle of a huge herd of elephants.

From his own travels and his personal contacts throughout much of Africa, Alfredo has acquired a sense of how well African game is doing in other regions. The picture he painted was gloomy. Central Africa? Not good. The Central African Republic, Sudan, Chad, Zaire, all hit hard by corruption and poaching. Elephants in Angola? "God knows what's left in Angola after years of civil war. Somalia, finished—civil war and chaos. Ethiopia, maybe something left, a few good tuskers." Uganda had been hit by the devastations of Idi Amin and many of the country's elephants have been slaughtered. Only recently has there been an increase in population. When I inquired about West Africa, he told me that the word is the forest elephants of Gabon are being hammered by poachers. And Kenya? "There is now at least a glimmer of hope with the Leakey appointment [as director of Kenya Wildlife Service]. He seems serious."

Alfredo had his own horror story to tell. "I was stuck in the mud last Christmas [1989] during the heavy rains in the western Serengeti, near my Grumeti River Camp. It was after dark and I could see more than a hundred flashlights in the distance, shining game. Poachers. They shot everything they could see—wildebeest, zebra, Tommy, Grant's [gazelles], topi. There are no elephants or lions left. No bushbuck." With a sigh, he added, "There is no hope for wildlife in Africa without sound management."

*   *   *

Serengeti. No other name has more allure, and certainly none has closer association with African wildlife than this vast plain in northern Tanzania. For those of America's television generation, there have been more public television programs and Marlin Perkins episodes about Serengeti than any other place in Africa.

I still have vivid recollection of my first trip to Serengeti, which borders Kenya and its Masai Mara Game Reserve. Descending on that winding dirt track on the western flank of Ngorongoro Crater, there is a spot where we pulled off to have lunch un-

A lone male elephant feeds alone in the misty dawn of Ngorongoro Crater in Tanzania. The downed trees, part of a forest of yellow-barked acacias, were probably knocked down by elephants, which feed on the bark and leaves.

A young elephant, approaching its teenage years, makes a bluff charge at our vehicles in Lake Manyara National Park in Tanzania.

der a broad acacia tree. Before us was a panorama extending into an infinity of yellow-green grassland and blue sky canopy. It was remarkable. One thin yellow track—the road—sliced across it. The rest was unmarred. I can only guess that this was what America's Great Plains must have looked like (*sans* road, of course) two hundred years ago when the Sioux and the Cheyenne and a million bison dominated the land. Here in Serengeti, it is the Masai and more than one million wildebeest and zebra, plus numerous other species more or less as they have been for a few millennia.

We camped that night at Naabi Hill in the eastern part of the six-thousand-square-mile Serengeti National Park. From the tent I heard hyenas giggling nearby and the scream of tree hyraxes. As usual I drank too much beer at supper and had to relieve a full bladder at 3:00 A.M. Unzipping the tent quietly, so as not to disturb others, I stumbled out into the darkness and walked thirty or forty feet away, whereupon I peed long and hard, shivering in the cold while looking up sleepily into a star-filled sky. Then back to the tent, almost missing it in the blackness of the moonless night. The next morning my guide informed me that he heard a tent unzip at 3:00 A.M. and he opened his own tent flap to peer outside. Shining his flashlight into the blackness, he spotted two large lions walking by. I did not drink any more beer at supper for the duration of our stay in Serengeti. It's easy to forget that there are still things here that will make a meal out of frail humans. On the other hand, it's nice to know that, in some respects, this wilderness has remained the same since the Pleistocene began. Or, as Edward Abbey once said, "It ain't really wilderness unless there's something out there that can eat you."

In a total of three trips to Serengeti I feel as though I've barely scratched the surface of this vast land. Most of my wanderings have been confined to the eastern and central portions of the park, from Naabi Hill and Ndutu to the Simba Kopjes and the lovely Seronera region, and to the Moru Kopjes with their colorful and mysterious Masai cave paintings. In January these eastern short-grass plains are filled with wildlife, and in mornings at Naabi Hill you poke your head out of your tent (checking, first, for lions) to watch the glow of dawn and to listen to the *onk, onk, onk* of ten thousand wildebeest and the braying of nearly that many zebras. I've driven the obscure tracks and watched cheetahs on a hunt, pausing to climb a kopje (literally, an island of rock in this sea of grass) to check out their territory and spot their prey. I've watched a lazy leopard sleeping while draped across the high branches of a yellow-barked acacia tree near the Seronera River. And I've seen the jumping mating dance of crested cranes in that same area. Once, near Simba Kopjes, I had the dubious honor of watching a pack of rare Cape hunting dogs, East Africa's most efficient hunter and most endangered species, chase down a Thomson gazelle and dismember it in seconds. On other occasions I've seen hyenas on a kill and a pride of lions feasting on a Cape buffalo, snarling and fighting for their turn at dinner. I've witnessed baby wildebeest, just born, as they stumble and fall in taking their first few steps of life. I've seen the rare Serval cat pounce on a guinea fowl, and vultures swoop in on the remains of a carcass to fight for space with the silver-backed jackals already scavenging the leftovers. I've seen giraffes silhouetted against a magnificent sunset. But I've seen very few elephants in Serengeti.

Part of it has to do with the fact that much of Serengeti is not particularly good elephant habitat. The name *Serengeti* is derived from the Masai and means "endless plains." It is a sea of grass in most places. I would be surprised, for example, to see elephants spending much time in the eastern portion of the park, for the endless grass here wouldn't have much to offer elephants. They do feed on grasses, but they prefer a variety of food—leaves and shoots of trees, reeds, brush. The prime elephant habitat in Serengeti is the rolling upland north of Banagi, more or less the northern-central part of the park. Here there's less grassland and more brush and scattered woodland—ideal elephant habitat. Unfortunately, this is near the region where most poaching has occurred.

Serengeti National Park has long had a history of poaching problems. But it has been meat and hides, not ivory, that has been the major target of poachers here. When the park was established in 1951 there were a number of small tribal groups living in the Serengeti region, hunting tribes who, for generations, had lived off the land and who, in more recent times, turned to killing for profit. The Wasukuma were particularly efficient and well organized, though it was the Wakuria who were the toughest to deal with and today remain a threat to both game and people in the northern reaches of Serengeti.

National park status made it illegal to kill game in Serengeti and in Tanzania's other national parks, but in the early years there was little enforcement. The park's establishment created a situation where, overnight, people who were subsistence hunters became criminal poachers. It took years of work on the part of people like Myles Turner, one of Serengeti's first wardens, to halt poaching activity and force the hunters to restrict their activities to areas outside the park. It was not an easy task, for there had been countless generations of such hunting carried on as tradition by the local people. Moreover, it was becoming increasingly profitable to sell the poached meat and hides. And as the world price of ivory soared, so did elephant poaching in Serengeti. As David Babu had pointed out to me earlier, Serengeti's elephant population has gone from four thousand to around four hundred in less than five years. Some of those missing elephants have undoubtedly migrated north into Kenya's Masai Mara Reserve where game is better protected from poaching and there is more suitable elephant habitat.

On one of my recent trips to Serengeti I did find a small herd of elephants between the Moru Kopjes and Seronera. They were nervous and fidgety. Hard to say whether it was because of poaching pressure or just their lack of familiarity with people. I hope it's the latter. But I hope, also, that Tanzania's new hard-nosed attitude on poaching continues and that Serengeti's elephants survive and thrive once again.

*　*　*

Ngorongoro Crater served as the model for the Garden of Eden. I'm convinced of it. Even today, with some game parks of Africa having been hammered by poaching and others overrun by tourists, Ngorongoro is like seeing Africa when it was young, fresh, pristine. This ten-mile-diameter caldera in northern Tanzania is one of the largest in the world. Ngorongoro was formed by an ancient volcanic eruption that blew the top off the volcano. The explosive gush of lava and cinders created a subterranean cavity, and when activity had ceased, the mountain fell in on itself to create the caldera. It is rimmed by high walls on all sides, and on the southern side it's a 2,500-foot plunge from crater rim to caldera floor. The whole effect is to create a natural barrier that inhibits human activity, particularly poaching, for reaching the rich game that inhabits the caldera requires a terrifying drive down one of the roughest roads I've seen in Africa—and back out again. (On a white-knuckle scale of one to ten, this road rates a good solid twelve in places!) Access by

Dawn in Ngorongoro Crater. Though hemmed in on all sides by the high walls of the crater, the game here does migrate in and out of the caldera to nearby regions of the Serengeti.

Lake Manyara National Park sits at the base of the Great Rift Valley, whose walls form one boundary. The lake, highly alkaline, is home to hundreds of thousands of flamingos. The park is composed of both groundwater forest and acacia forests.

foot is equally hard. But game does migrate into and out of the crater, moving to and from the nearby Serengeti ecosystem and adjacent areas.

Why is it the Garden of Eden? I've never seen another place, in Africa or elsewhere, that has the feel of primeval beauty that's found in Ngorongoro. The bottom of the caldera has an incredibly diverse habitat. There's dense forest of yellow-barked acacias, short-grass grasslands, fresh water springs at Ngoitokitok, a saline lake replete with thousands of pink flamingos, and moist rain forest on the upper slopes of the crater. The density of wildlife is astounding. Everywhere you turn are thousands of wildebeest and zebra. Virtually everywhere you go and everywhere you look there are animals of one species or another: gazelles, both Grant's and Thomson's in abundance, hippos, hyenas in quantity, jackals, lions, Cape buffalo, one of the last great concentrations of black rhino left. And, of course, elephants.

There does not appear to be a large population of elephants at Ngorongoro, at least, not in the caldera itself. It's also curious that the ones who inhabit the crater floor are mostly males — large males. Some of the biggest tusked elephants I've seen in Africa are residents of Ngorongoro Crater, a sign that poaching hasn't been much of a problem here. And as further evidence of that, many of these big males are quite placid in the presence of people in vehicles. I've had them approach my Land Rover as closely as a dozen feet or less, grazing unconcernedly. A good thing, for one of them had a set of enormous tusks and could have wreaked incredible damage on both vehicle and people, had he chosen.

Where are the females and families, I asked one of the rangers. On the rim, he said. In the denser forests high above the caldera bottom. But what about females who are ready for mating? The ranger laughed. "*Bwana ndovu*, the *dume* [male], he must walk a long way to make love to mama." It's a tough hike. Might explain why there's a relatively low population density here.

On my last trip to Ngorongoro I watched two *dumes* sparring, intertwining trunks, backing off, thrusting and parrying with their long, massive tusks. The sound of tusk clacking against tusk and the sight of two giants in battle, albeit mock battle, was something of another geologic era. Long after the light had faded and it was too dim for photographs, I watched in fascination. It will be a tragedy if these magnificent animals disappear from the earth.

KENYA

The Cessna 310 lifted off the hot runway at Nairobi's Wilson Airport, banked sharply to the right over Nairobi National Park, and climbed into the clear air. As we turned and gained altitude, the land below presented itself in paradoxical mosaic. Thomson's and Grant's gazelles and occasional giraffes dotted the green of the park below, while not far away were the crowded slums, the shacks that housed the growing numbers of impoverished people flocking to Nairobi in hopes of work. The tin roofs, glinting in the sunlight, resembled a wave about to wash over the tall hotels and office buildings of Nairobi's center. As we headed north the density of population dropped exponentially; the land was green with coffee plantations and wheat farms and pineapple crops, criss-crossed with roads, yellow and orange etchings given color by the volcanic soil. Though less densely populated than the big city, there was still a feeling that humanity is making more and more demands on this earth. Smaller plots of land, the *shambas*, were increasingly evident, each with a glinting tin roof and furrows of hope plowed into the rich soil. Off the right wingtip was Thika, made famous by Elspeth Huxley in her classic *The Flame Trees of Thika*.

We headed northwest. The flat land soon took on contours and relief and the verdancy changed from the light green of agriculture to the cool, dark green of unbroken forest as we approached the Aberdares. As the plane banked sharply, I could see waterfalls in the creases of canyons and then open slopes of heath lands on the higher elevations of the mountain range. I saw no game. But even elephants are hidden by the thick forest cover. Most evident were the park's boundaries, visible in most places by the sharp distinction of cultivated lands on one side and wilderness forest on the other. Even here we humans press in ever closer.

We flew over the famed Treetops safari lodge and the town of Mweiga, and then over Naro Moru where I had stayed on occasion. Ahead of us loomed Mt. Kenya, a sharp, jagged volcanic peak sitting on the equator and clad with gleaming snowfields and glaciers. *Kirinyaga* was the name given this 17,156-foot peak by the Kikuyu who also called it the "House of God." It does, indeed, appear to be a holy place.

North of Mt. Kenya the land suddenly drops — almost three thousand feet in about twenty miles. From the central highlands, averaging a cool six thousand feet above sea level, the transition is startling. Green turns to yellow and brown, the hot desert lands of the Rift Valley and the beginning of the Northern Frontier District. As we flew past Isiolo, I strained to see familiar landmarks in the Samburu/Buffalo Springs Reserves where I had spent much time. I could make out the blood-red, green-rimmed course of Ewaso Nyiro, the major river bisecting the two adjacent reserves. In moments we touched down in a cloud of dust on the airstrip in Shaba National Reserve, which lies east of, and nearly contiguous with, Samburu/Buffalo Springs.

This region seems an unlikely place for much wildlife. It is dry, crackling, and fiercely hot, like something out of the American southwest. In many places the stony soil supports little grass. Thorny brush and sparse acacia trees dominate the landscape. However, like our Southwest, it is a land of haunting beauty. The colors range from black basalt of lava flows to colorful rhyolite hills, all fringed

Family groups feed on the lush grasses nurtured by springs in Kenya's Amboseli National Park. The springs are fed from subterranean water from melting snows on Mt. Kilimanjaro, 19,340 feet in elevation in the background.

A family group heads for a water hole in the last rays of sunlight at Amboseli National Park. Shortly after the sun sank below the horizon, members of the group began to trumpet loudly and run crazily through the brush — all in play.

with enough greenery for contrast. Some valleys and arroyos are thick with lovely yellow grasses. And in the distance looms Lolokwe, the sacred mountain to the Samburu people, a granitic massif whose great cliffs glow with crimson and orange at dawn and again at sunset. For the most part it is desert, and for desert rats like myself, it has great appeal, wildlife or not.

Yet there is game here, a surprising amount. The reason is water. Fed by the rain-gathering Laikipia Plateau to the southwest, the Ewaso Nyiro ("Red River" in Samburu language) maintains a steady flow of life-giving water throughout most of the year. Where there is water there is vegetation: lush grasses, yellow-barked acacia (fever trees), borassus and doum palms, dense brush, reeds, thick grasses, all in junglelike profusion that follows the twisting river in a corridor about a quarter mile wide. Where there is vegetation there are herbivores, and where there are herbivores there are carnivores. Thus a rich and diverse community of life exists here in a blend of riverine and desert ecosystems.

Most of the animal life does not confine itself to this green corridor, but ranges out over large areas of dry lands. Some, like the gerenuk, a sleek, long-necked member of the gazelle family, do not require water. Instead they manage to derive what moisture they need by browsing on dry, prickly bushes and trees, often standing on hind feet to reach leaves and stems. But most of the larger mammals eventually return to the river to slake thirsts. And the elephants move daily from their feeding areas to nearby springs or marshes or the river itself.

In several years of visits to Samburu/Buffalo Springs, I haven't noticed any obvious signs of diminishing elephant population. There always seem to be numerous family units in the forests and grassy wetlands bordering the Ewaso Nyiro.

I had never been to Shaba before, though I knew about its most famous resident, Joy Adamson, author of *Born Free,* who was at work on a program of reintroducing leopards to the wild at the time of her murder in 1980. The easternmost of these three clustered reserves, Shaba, I was told, had suffered more from *shifta* poaching than the others. It was said to have been "stiff with game" a decade ago. Its

Cattle egrets follow elephants and feed on insects disturbed by their grazing. Elephants use their trunks for feeding, drinking, smelling for danger, and for touching and expressing affection to other elephants.

This little guy, less than a year old, seems delighted in his mischievousness — bugging the hell out of a sleeping brother or sister. Masai Mara National Reserve.

locale put it in line with routes that might be taken by Somali moving to the interior of Kenya from the border about 150 miles to the east.

Almost two days of exploring Shaba seemed to confirm the fact that game was sparse. Six elephants were spotted. All were bachelors, medium to large males with small or broken tusks. Puzzling to me, however, was the fact that they did not seem particularly disturbed by presence of the Land Rover; one would suspect that being under siege by poachers would make them extremely wary of vehicles with people. Instead they moved about placidly, feeding on grasses and brush.

Other game was sparse as well, another sign of heavy poaching activity. Poachers do not confine themselves to elephants, even though that may be their primary and most lucrative prey. Anything that can be sold for meat or hide is taken. In particular, the beautiful and rare Grevy's zebra, found only in this region, brings a good price for its hide on the black market. And many animals such as giraffe and impala are shot for food while the poachers are camped in the wilds.

Shaba does not have the numbers of tourists that come to Samburu/Buffalo Springs. I'm not sure whether it's due to the fact that game has become sparse or because it's lesser known. A paucity of tourism could contribute to increased poaching. In parks such as Amboseli, where enormous numbers of people flock each year, the elephants have been relatively free of poaching activity. With the presence of large numbers of people, poachers risk a greater chance of detection and apprehension. But in Shaba, with few visitors, the hunters have less chance of being detected.

It's possible, also, that elephants and certain other game, feeling the pressure of hunting, have moved to more secure areas such as Samburu/Buffalo Springs. Elephants, in particular, are more intelligent than we've realized in the past. From their standpoint, carloads of jabbering, camera-clicking people are preferable to deadly gun-toting *shifta*.

Perhaps the tourism situation in Shaba will change. The new Serova Lodge was completed in 1989, a facility replete with air-conditioned rooms, a turquoise, free-form swimming pool, and solar heating panels that provide an abundance of hot water. The landscaping is spectacular, with native palms and shrubs, pools and waterfalls, and dazzling flowers. There's even a little pond with a baby crocodile that snaps at passing tourists, though, of course, if you care for the larger man-eating cousins, they lurk along the banks of the Ewaso Nyiro a hundred yards away. It's a beautiful place, but during my stay it was eerily empty. Perhaps with more tourism, the game will have a chance to recover here. Of course, with little game it might be difficult to attract tourists. An ecological Catch-22.

*   *   *

For the next couple of days I moved across the road to Samburu/Buffalo Springs, the "road" being that dusty, washboard track that heads north after leaving the pavement at Isiolo and bisects the parched country of the Northern Frontier, past Samburu and Buffalo Springs, through Marsabit Reserve, and finally to the border of Ethiopia. No-man's-land, north of here, mysterious, still replete with dangers to travelers, yet appealing and luring. No, actually, it isn't a no-man's-land, for that implies that no one lives here. Despite the savage heat and brittle, blowing desert, it is home to a number of people like the Turkana, pastoralists who herd their cattle wherever a blade or two of grass might be found. There are also the El Molo, tall, powerfully built fishermen from the shores of Lake Turkana. The Rendille live in the rocky wastes around Marsabit where they herd their camels. Samburu people, whose traditional lands range from Lake Turkana to the Ewaso Nyiro, are closely related to Masai and share their language and cultural heritage. And then there are Somali, who also herd camels. Many Somali people migrated to Kenya when forced to leave their homeland because of drought and civil war. They now live peacefully in this Northern Frontier District. Only a relative few of them have turned to poaching.

A fascinating region. Someday I'll explore it, but for now I settled in comfort at a tented lodge in Samburu, situated on the shore of the Ewaso Nyiro. There had been a lot of rain this year on the Laikipia, for the river was high. It hissed by the shore like a vermilion snake, wide and deep with shifting waves. I was reminded of the Colorado River back in the days before it had been so extensively dammed and it ran red with sediment, rich in iron,

A family drinks from the Ewaso Nyiro ("Red River" in the Samburu language) in Samburu National Reserve in northern Kenya. The youngster is probably a week old or less.

Cynthia Moss, in Amboseli National Park. Beginning her now-famous studies of Amboseli's elephants in 1972, Cynthia has become one of the world's foremost experts on the African elephant.

At a salt lick in Aberdare National Park, an elephant uses its tusks to loosen the salt-laden soil to eat.

"too thick to drink, too thin to plow." Some years, however, this "Red River" of Samburu dries up, creating problems for the animals and forcing them to congregate around the springs and seeps nearby. There seemed little danger of that this year.

During the years 1973 to 1977, elephant population in Samburu/Buffalo Springs Reserves plunged drastically from an estimated 2,500 to about five hundred. The *shifta* were busy; they had been since before the establishment of the reserves in 1966. In fact, during those early years few travelers came here because the Somalis dominated this land and made it dangerous to travel. They even attacked the town of Isiolo, killing the district commissioner. It's safe to travel here now, though there's still a feeling of stepping back in time to the frontier days of our American West, but with elephants and zebras and giraffes roaming the wide open spaces in place of the deer, the antelope, and the bison.

Since that massive slaughter of the early 1970s, the elephant population has increased slightly, with the number now estimated at about seven hundred. Stepped-up antipoaching patrols and a sizable number of tourists have made poaching difficult here.

In the days I spent at Samburu and Buffalo Springs, and during another visit a few weeks later, I noted quite a contrast to Shaba. There were numerous family units of elephants, mostly numbering about eight to ten in size. They stuck to areas of forest and marshlands near the Ewaso Nyiro and seemed not at all disturbed by the presence of vehicles. I watched in fascination as one family moved past, leaving a large meadow where they had been grazing, and headed into thick forest and brush. With barely a glance in my direction, they lumbered by—three large females, four subadults (I couldn't determine the sex because of the brush), and two youngsters of about two to three years in age. They seemed to march with a purpose, though I couldn't tell what it was. Perhaps they'd had their fill of grasses and reeds and now looked forward to some succulent leaves and branches of trees. There were numerous trees on the other side of the river that had been killed by elephants, stark, silvery forms that stood boldly against the blue sky.

When the family reached the edge of forest there was no searching for a route. They simple pushed their way into the foliage and instantly disappeared. Were it not for the cracking noise they made tramping through undergrowth, I would never have known they were there. And in a moment the noise ceased. The river was a mere fifty yards on the other side of the trees from where they had entered. But there was simply no way of telling that there were nine large animals in that small section of forest.

On another day I had stopped on a track to watch a family group work its way toward us. They moved slowly, with purpose, probably headed for a favorite spot on the river. One female had a *toto* (baby) not more than a week old. It trotted along clumsily, still a little uncertain on its feet. But it seemed in a playful mood, swinging its head from side to side with its trunk waving straight out like a rubber hose. The sunlight made the ears glow pink.

When mama came closer, it became obvious that my vehicle was in her chosen path, and with a newborn, I grew more apprehensive about her maternal protectiveness. When she was about ten yards from us she paused, raised her trunk, and shook her head from side to side. "Outta the way, bipeds." Lidede, my guide, quickly started the engine (I think he had his hand on the ignition key as he watched the elephants approach), jammed it in reverse, and backed up ten fast yards. With the youngster safely by her side, away from us, mama continued on her way. Rule Number One: Elephants always have right-of-way.

Later that day I encountered the same group and the same mama made us back up again—this time because she wanted to feed on a clump of vegetation around the tree we had parked next to. (There was plenty of vegetation all around, but I think she wanted to assert herself again.) *Hakuna matata.* (No problem.) We moved back about ten yards and she and *toto* began feeding. Actually, she was feeding and the baby was playing at feeding (youngsters that age suckle exclusively). It wound its miniature trunk around grasses and leaves, trying to grasp them but having no luck in imitating mama. That damned appendage didn't seem to work properly. Finally, in frustration, it tripped back to mom's forelegs, curled its trunk over its head to get it out of the way, and suckled long and hard.

* * *

Ian and Jane Craig live on a hilltop in a stonework house, topped with hand-hewn beams and a thatched roof. Their view is as spectacular as any in Kenya, looking out over a broad green valley of mixed grassland and large, yellow-barked acacia trees. This particular species of acacia is the largest

Part of a family group in Amboseli National Park. Females remain with the family group for life. Males leave the family at twelve to fourteen years of age to strike out on their own.

This female, part of a family group I was photographing in Masai Mara, picked up this stick and began playing with it—putting it in her mouth, twirling it around with her trunk. When the group moved on, she followed, still holding her plaything in her mouth.

"Oh yeah? My old man can whip your old man." Actually, this is a display not of aggression, but of affection. Part of a large family group, these two simply walked up to each other and touched heads together.

Taking a dust bath, Amboseli National Park. Elephants seem to love covering themselves with dust, water, or mud. Though their hides are thick, the dust and mud probably help to minimize irritation by tick bites. And it's probably just plain fun.

Masai Mara National Reserve. Elephants often greet each other by touching.

of several varieties found in East Africa, and, I think, the loveliest. The yellow-green bark contains chlorophyll, which aids in photosynthesis during times when the tree has shed its leaves. The trees stand tall, some thirty to forty feet in height, with a broad, graceful canopy of branches and leaves that resembles a large umbrella. Elephants love to eat the bark, which they sometimes strip off in long ribbons after first loosening it with their tusks. In the earliest days of European exploration, this tree was named the "fever tree" because parties that camped under such trees often came down with malarial fever. They never realized that, because the tree grows in wetter areas, the source of their fever was not the tree but malaria-bearing mosquitoes that thrive in the dampness.

Capping the view from the Craigs' balcony is *Kirinyaga,* Mt. Kenya, about thirty miles to the south. From this angle the mountain bristles with basaltic spires.

They call their place Lewa Downs. It's a forty-two-thousand-acre (sixty-six-square-mile) private game-and-cattle ranch, with nearly two hundred resident elephants. In addition to these, another two thousand elephants move through here, roaming extensively over parts of the Laikipia Plateau. It's the largest assemblage of elephants outside of the parks and game reserves in Kenya.

Are there problems with poachers? "We get them coming down from the northern boundary of the ranch, which is unfenced," Ian said. As protection, there are sixty-four men in the employ of the ranch, with ten of them armed and trained shooters. One five-man anti-poaching team patrols the northern boundary to intercept any potential poachers. The men are hand-picked, experienced in the bush — Turkana, Wandorobo, Wakamba. The result has been few, if any, elephant kills on the ranch.

Not long ago Ian had been witness to the slaughter of some elephants in the Matthews Range about eighty miles north of Lewa Downs by *shifta,* some wearing military-style uniforms, others dressed in Somali *kikoys,* the sarong-like cloths wrapped around the waist. Ian's party were too few in num-

An older female with a very young calf, perhaps only a week or two old, is accompanied by a younger female—perhaps a daughter.

ber and too poorly armed to engage the poachers, so they watched from a distant hillside with binoculars as the Somali gunned down five elephants with automatic weapons, Kalishnikovs (AK-47's), he thought. They ran and fired for forty-five minutes, chasing a herd. Undoubtedly other elephants were wounded and probably died later. The poachers then chopped out the tusks with axes and carried the ivory into a small valley with dense brush where they were out of sight for a while.

When finally the *shifta* left, without the ivory, Ian and his party carefully moved down to the copse to attempt to find the booty. "We searched it for two bloody hours—and this with Dorobo trackers, mind you, the best in the business—and never found a tusk. They're bloody good, I'll tell you."

Later I accompanied Ian on a drive around part of Lewa Downs. The eastern and southern boundaries have a twelve-foot-high electric fence, which, as Ian explains, "keeps our rhinos—fifteen of them now—from wandering off the ranch, where they'd be killed in no time, and alerts our main headquar-

ters back at the house if anyone tries to cut it or climb it." To demonstrate, Ian contacted headquarters with his radio and had the transmit key there left open while he placed a foot on one of the wire strands. Over the radio could be heard the squeal of an alarm. Impressive. But costly?

"Bloody pricey, to be sure, but it's the only way to keep the poor *kifaru* [rhino] safe from poachers," he said. As for the elephants, they seem secure enough right now. And not being used to tourists, as park elephants are, those at Lewa can be a little *mkorofi* ("bad-tempered" in Swahili) as we discovered by following one big male along a dirt track in the Land Rover. When we approached a little too closely, he swung around quickly with ears flared and made a threatening gesture toward us. Back off, he seemed to say. We did. One does not argue with five tons of angry elephant.

*　　*　　*

About ten miles north of the northern boundary of Aberdare National Park, the equator slices across

Kenya. One would think that, lying so close to the equator, the Aberdares would have a hot and steamy climate. But evenings here are brisk, and in the mornings at our camp in the forest we sipped our steaming cups of coffee around a warming campfire. Bundled in sweaters and jackets, we watched, through the trees, as the dawn sun etched the edges of Mt. Kenya with light.

The camp arrangement had been handled by Bill Winter, long-time safari outfitter and former Kenya game warden. The bright green tents blended well with the lush foliage and brush. The little clearing was hemmed in tightly by the vegetation, though game trails radiated out into the forest. However, Bill warned that it would be best not to stray too far afoot. There are lions and leopards about, you know. Or, even worse, buffalo. Probably more deaths in Kenya can be attributed to buffalo than to all the big cats put together. Big, mean-tempered, and unpredictable, their sharp, re-curved horns are deadly weapons. Surprising one at close range in the brush could be fatal.

I heeded the warning, keeping a sharp eye out on each trip to the loo at the edge of camp. Our primary interest was not buffalo, but the elephants and how well they were doing here in the Aberdares. With me were writer Bob Jones and Dan Gerber, poet and novelist. Both had spent time in the Aberdares many years earlier and both had memories of numerous elephants here. Earlier, before arriving at camp, we had visited John Muhanga, senior park warden for Aberdares, at the park headquarters in Mweiga. He had assured us that poaching had been light in the park and that there were increased antipoaching patrols. As evidence of the new hard-nosed policy against poaching, when we stopped at the park entrance gate we were greeted by a ranger sporting a large white button that read BURN THE IVORY, KILL THE POACHERS.

This is a different kind of habitat for elephants. The Aberdare Range, called *Nyandarua* by the Kikuyu, is part of the upland interior of central Kenya and forms part of the eastern wall of the Rift Valley. West of here lies Wanjohi, the notorious "Happy Valley" made famous by the book and movie *White Mischief* about the excesses of the British settlers in the 1930s. Within the park elevations range from seven thousand to over thirteen thousand feet and, because of this, the climate is cooler and wetter. Much of the park is covered with ancient cedar forest and Hagenia trees, the latter the same species

found in the mountain gorilla domain of the Virunga Volcanoes in Rwanda and Zaire. It's thick and lush, with black-and-white colubus monkeys leaping among branches high in the trees, buffalo and bushbuck, and the rare forest hog in the thick undergrowth. It's also home to about two thousand elephants (down from about three thousand in 1973) that roam within the 311 square miles of the park, ranging from rain forest to the moorlands above timberline.

For the next few days we drove many of the *njias* (dirt roads and tracks) within the park, finding numerous elephants. Compared to the big-tusked elephants of Amboseli and Tsavo, these had very small tusks. The females, in particular, had tusks that were very thin and often curved at odd angles. Because the forest is so thick, the elephants use the *njias* themselves to move about easily, making for some exciting encounters when you round a bend and find the way blocked by a large family of elephants. Some of the family matriarchs were a little *mkorofi,* standing ground and refusing to get off the track. Rule Number Two: Elephants *always* have right-of-way.

While direct attacks on elephants by poachers may be ebbing, there are still some indirect threats. From the air I had seen how the park is pressured by civilization. Farms press against the fenced boundary in many places. And people in areas nearby may steal into the park to set traps and snares for meat, catching smaller animals like bushbuck. Even this can have some impact on elephants, as we discovered one evening.

The sun had just set behind the higher peaks to the west and the forest slipped into shadow. Bill was headed back to camp when he discovered a new *njia*—really just a set of tracks leading into the forest—that we hadn't explored. He wheeled the Land Rover onto it. The path was narrow and branches slapped at the sides of the vehicle as we bounced along. In a few hundred yards we found some elephants grazing on a hillside and we stopped to watch. The brush was thick and we could barely make them out. As we looked into the fading twilight, a forest hog, fat and bristling with long black hairs, stepped out of the brush in front of the Land Rover. A rare sight; the forest hog was the last large mammal of Africa to be discovered by scientists in 1907. I took a few pictures, but the sound of the camera made it nervous and soon it darted off into the brush.

Kuki Gallman at the edge of Makutano Gorge on her Ol Ari Nyiro Ranch on the Laikipia Plateau of central Kenya.

In another quarter mile the forest opened up into a grassy swale with a stream running through it. Here we found another family of elephants, led by a big matriarch. She flared her ears and, while the others hastened across the road to seek shelter in the forest, she stood her ground against us, trunk up-raised. It was then that I noticed her injury. About a foot up from the tip of her trunk was a terrible gash that had nearly severed it. There was no bleeding to indicate that it was a fresh wound. But it hadn't healed, and probably wouldn't. Bill shook his head sadly. "A cable snare. Probably set by meat poachers," he said. "She probably can't drink properly, if at all. And it's so bad that using her trunk to eat is too painful. Poor old girl. She'll probably starve to death." She moved on to join her family and we headed into the deepening darkness of the forest and the night.

*   *   *

"Careful, Boyd, he may charge." Bob Jones was standing about ten yards behind me when he issued the warning in a low voice, trying not to startle the big bull elephant. "He's *mkorofi*—mad as hell," said Bill Winter standing next to Bob. "Get ready to run."

I wasn't sure I wanted to run just yet. I had walked on ahead with the chief game scout for Ol Ari Nyiro Ranch, an old Borana tribesman named Hussein Omar, who carried a big .458 caliber Winchester for protection. I wanted to get a better angle for pictures of the elephants gathered around the watering tank. The big bull was in musth. The side of his massive head was stained by the fluid issuing from temporal glands. Pumped up on testosterone, he was acting nervously about our presence. I was equally pumped up—on adrenaline.

When I moved beyond the brush into the open, I hunkered down with elbows on knees to brace the camera. Through the three hundred millimeter lens, not a particularly long telephoto, the bull loomed large in the viewfinder. As I started shooting, the *bzzzt, bzzzt,* of the camera's motor drive seemed to alarm the bull even more. With ears waving at right

107

angles to his head, he lifted his trunk and let out a loud, blaring trumpet. Hairs on the back of my neck stood up, but I kept shooting. Perhaps I was concentrating too much on the images in the viewfinder, for in seconds the bull began to close the gap between us. Suddenly the image was completely filled with a gray blur and Hussein was frantically waving at me to move back quickly. I backed up, still shooting, trying to get Hussein in the foreground of the picture and the bull in back. Then, as the elephant quickened his charge, Bill Winter clapped his hands sharply three times. ("An old bushman's trick," Bill said later.) The bull stopped, startled, about thirty feet from us. He raised his trunk once again, gave a shrill trumpet, then turned and walked back unhurriedly to the other elephants who had been milling about watching the episode unfold.

We moved quickly back to the Land Rover parked about fifty yards away, and as I climbed inside, that last spurt of adrenaline began to wear off. My hands quaked as I rewound the film in the camera.

Kuki Gallman is an enchanting, green-eyed, honey-blonde for whom Kenya has been a source of infinite pleasure and great pain. She moved to Kenya in 1972, the wife of Italian industrialist Paolo Gallman. Soon after, her brother-in-law was killed in a hunting accident by a wounded elephant. Then Paolo died in an automobile accident on his way home from the coast. In 1983 her seventeen-year-old son, Immanuele, a budding herpetologist, was bitten by a puff adder. He died in her arms.

"If I was meant to leave Africa," she said, "I'd have left then." She stayed. Today her one-hundred-thousand-acre ranch, Ol Ari Nyiro, is devoted to saving forty-six rhino and about three hundred to one thousand elephants that move through the area each year. She also has about six thousand cattle and sheep for the commercial side of the operation.

In honor of her late husband and son, Kuki established the Gallman Memorial Foundation for the purpose of preserving the wildlife on her ranch and adjacent areas of the Laikipia Plateau. We talked about her plans as she showed us a favorite spot of hers, a steep, spectacular gorge called *Mkutano* (Swahili for "Meeting Place"). As I looked into its depths and caught a glimpse of Lake Baringo's shimmering waters in the distance, she told us of her explorations of the gorge. "We found many stone artifacts in the gorge and there are many caves down there. It's awesome, in the old sense of the word, to

A youngster, perhaps a month old, awakens from a nap and stands up in Masai Mara National Reserve.

A lone male takes a drink from Ewaso Nyiro in Samburu National Reserve in Kenya. The trunk is a useful appendage, functioning for drinking, gathering food, smelling enemies, touching and expressing affection toward other elephants, and for taking dust and mud baths.

An old male rubs his trunk on a dead tree in Masai Mara National Reserve. The tree may have been killed by elephants, stripped of bark, and pushed over to allow feeding on leaves.

think that I am part of a continuity in this place dating back to the Pleistocene and earlier. One in which humankind and wildlife shared this place, indeed the entire planet at one time, in mutual harmony. I'm doing what I can to keep it that way, at least here."

* * *

Amboseli is the quintessential African national park, fulfilling the vision that people seem to have, rightly or wrongly, of East Africa. Located in southern Kenya, adjacent to Tanzania, Amboseli sits at the base of Mt. Kilimanjaro. The gleaming, snow-capped, 19,344-foot mountain towers over the green savannahs of both countries. It's undoubtedly the most impressive backdrop of any park in the world.

In addition to Kilimanjaro, Amboseli is noted for its hordes of tourists dressed in silly safari outfits, its herds of heavy-tusked elephants, and Cynthia Moss. The last two items are closely related, for Cynthia has spent eighteen years here, to become one of the world's foremost experts on elephants.

Amboseli's elephant population, about seven hundred total, has remained remarkably stable for nearly twenty years. Actually, depending on the accuracy of the figures, there has been a slight increase in that time span, where most other reserves and parks have shown drastic declines in elephant populations.

Part of this can probably be attributed to Amboseli's popularity as a tourist destination. The airstrip here is busy, with numerous flights bringing hordes of tourists from Mombasa, Malindi, and Nairobi, to be picked up by flocks of minivans that speed about in search of game for the clients. The safari lodges are always full, brimming with Italians, Germans, French, and Americans. On a recent trip there I was jostled about in the mobbed terrace of Amboseli Lodge by scores of 7-Up bottlers from America, the top sellers who had been given a free safari as a prize for their salesmanship. As much as I abhor crowded parks, I must admit that tourism has been responsible for maintaining much game, particularly keeping elephants here free of poach-

This toto *(baby) in Samburu National Reserve is probably only a day or two old. It tried to grasp some grasses with its trunk but had little control over this strange appendage. Learning to use the trunk takes time.*

ing. No poacher would stand a chance of popping an elephant unseen and making off with tusks with so many tourist-packed minivans scampering about. At times it's even difficult to take a photograph without the ubiquitous vehicle in the picture.

Despite the crowds, this has been an important locale for elephant research. Cynthia Moss came to Amboseli in 1972 to begin her now-famous studies on the lives of elephants, their families, relationships, mating, and survival from drought, poachers, disease, injuries, and even how they cope with tourism. Her book, *Elephant Memories,* has become, alongside the work of the Douglas-Hamiltons, the important reference on elephants.

Cynthia's camp is in a meadow surrounded by borassis palms and yellow-barked acacia trees, with a marvelous view of Kilimanjaro from her tent. Elephants come here to graze in the lush grasses.

"I woke up this morning and heard a lion roar. It was exciting—that's the first I'd heard in weeks," she said as we sat in her spacious tent. Why is that so unusual, I asked. I'd often heard lions roaring in many game parks and reserves. "The Masai," she replied. "They've been poisoning the lions. They killed seven about eighteen months ago. Lion sightings have become rare here."

What has been the impact of Masai on elephants? "There's still a certain amount of harassment and spearing by young Masai trying to prove their manhood. It hasn't been without a price. Two Masai have been killed recently, one trying to spear an elephant, the other a child herding cattle." Overall, however, the elephants have learned to smell and hear Masai and to run off. But it has limited the movement of elephants and tends to make them cluster in the park where they are free from harassment.

I asked her about arguments put forth by southern African countries that their surplus of elephants, by the cropping and selling of ivory, helps to pay for more game management and conservation. She had an obvious distaste for that philosophy. "In southern Africa," she said, "they have a different approach toward game—a more intensive management. It's more like ranching. They drill for water, build dams, and basically manage the animals as a cash crop, like cattle. In East Africa, the philosophy is to

set aside natural ecosystems, more like America does with wilderness areas and national parks. Even at that, elephants in Amboseli make more money from tourism than the sale of ivory makes for Zimbabwe. And they stay alive."

In the region of Amboseli, elephants range over about four hundred square miles of ecosystem suitable for them. But the park itself embraces only about 150 square miles. The remaining surrounding lands are part of Masai group ranches, divided among clans. Changes in traditional Masai pastoralist culture are in the offing. A day before meeting with Cynthia Moss I had met some young Masai, and talked with them through an interpreter. They spoke about plans to subdivide one or more of the group ranches, to give land to the younger people coming of age. The smaller parcels could not sustain cattle grazing to any extent and probably would be used for farming, something that heretofore had never been practiced by Masai. These young people with whom I spoke wore the traditional, colorful shukas and carried their spears, but they also wore Adidas shoes and Casio watches.

I asked Cynthia about the growing population and the schemes for more farms. "If massive agricultural development occurs," she said, "there's no hope for wildlife."

Driving back to camp that afternoon, I watched a sizable herd of elephants, probably more than one family group, as they moved slowly across scrub and grasslands toward a water hole. Suddenly a couple of them began running, trumpeting loudly. Soon the whole herd was running, heads and trunks in the air, ears flapping, blaring out loud trumpets. I thought, at first, that something had frightened them or that some fighting was occurring among them. But as I watched, I decided that it must be some form of play or expression of joy. They raised clouds of dust, and the cacophony continued as they pranced toward their water hole. Even the youngsters were caught up in the excitement, running with bobbing heads, waving their trunks. The last rays of sunlight painted the top of Kilimanjaro's snows a pale lavender.

When I returned to camp at dark, I could still hear trumpeting in the distance.

A family group, led by the old matriarch on the right, challenges us on one of the narrow njias *in Aberdare National Park. Because of the thick forest cover, elephants use these dirt tracks to move about in the park.*

THE LAST
DAYS OF EDEN

This we know: The earth does not belong to man; man belongs to the earth. All things are connected like the blood that unites us all. Man did not weave the web of life, he is merely a strand in it. Whatever he does to the web, he does to himself. —Chief Seattle, Suquamish Indians chief, 1854. Joseph Campbell Power of Myth.

*   *   *

Abdi Omar Bashir has fire in his eyes, a blaze of anger that spells trouble for poachers. In his crisply starched uniform, he stood before a large map of Kenya in his office at Langata, the headquarters of Kenya Wildlife Service, located at the entrance to Nairobi National Park. "We have good information from informers and we know the routes taken by the *shifta* from Somalia across the Tana and Galana rivers." He used a ruler to slap at the map, pointing to those places where, he hoped, his troops would intercept the poachers. His dark eyes flashed each time he made a point. Bashir, forty-six years old, tall and lean, was well prepared for this role, having spent twenty-four years in Kenya's paramilitary General Service Unit, the last part of it as commandant. Now he is Richard Leakey's deputy director of enforcement for Kenya Wildlife Service.

Bashir's appointment came in November of 1989 as part of the campaign to clean up corruption in the wildlife department. It was no secret that for years gate guards and clerks at national parks were skimming off receipts and that park rangers were often involved in poaching activities directly or, indirectly, taking payoffs from poachers to turn a blind eye to the activities.

No more. "My first priority is to clean things up," Bashir said with conviction. His power to do so comes not only from Leakey, but from Kenya's president, Daniel arap Moi. "I've been recruiting game scouts from the northern tribes—Rendille, Samburu, Wanderobo, Turkana, and Borana." These, he pointed out, are people who know the bush country as well as any *shifta*. There would be no more citified recruits who had little knowledge of surviving in the harsh wilderness. He has even enlisted the aid of captured *shifta,* turning them into game scouts.

"We need more good weapons, good radios, fast transport on the land and in the air," said Bashir. "We need good discipline and good dedication. We've got good men now, and we can win this war. We *will* win it. I promise you that this will be done." His eyes flashed again as he slapped the palm of his hand with the ruler. I almost saluted.

The war on poaching has taken on a new dimension with the appointment of people like Bashir and the continued work of Bill Woodley and others. But it is Richard Leakey who has restored confidence in Kenya's ability to save its game.

Leakey's spacious office at Langata has photographs of rhino and elephants, the two most threatened species in East Africa. There are two phones that ring almost constantly. For a man that had a kidney transplant ten years earlier, he has thrown himself into this job with incredible energy. An admitted workaholic, surviving on four hours' sleep a night, he is on the move constantly. An earlier meeting with him didn't materialize because he had taken off in his single-engine Cessna for Meru National Park in the north and had to spend the night there. Sometimes, for relaxation, he drops in on his world-famous archaeological site, Koobi Fora, on the

On July 18, 1989, $3 million worth of confiscated ivory was burned by Kenya as demonstration of that country's commitment to halt poaching and illicit trade in ivory. (Photo © by Steve Turner)

northeast shore of Lake Turkana, just to see how things are going and to visit for a while with the two-million-year-old ancestors he and his team have discovered there. ("Some executives play golf for relaxation," he has joked in the past. "I look for fossils.") He's equally at home in government offices of London or Washington where he works tirelessly at raising funds for his efforts in Kenya and lobbies for worldwide policies to halt ivory trading.

"We have an obligation here in Kenya to maintain our bio-diversity," he said when I finally caught up with him. "But we also have to recognize that the era of free-ranging game in Africa is finished. Outside the parks and reserves, it is as unrealistic to have wild animals running loose as it is in your American suburbs. Wildlife, if it is to survive in Africa, must pay its own way from now on."

Among his strategies is a plan to raise entry fees in the national parks and to share more of those revenues with local people. When local people benefit from tourist income, he argues, there will be much stronger and more widespread support to preserve the animals that people come to see.

However, Leakey foresees problems of the kind that have occurred in our national parks — overuse and overcrowding. "Our parks are taking a beating from tourists. We will begin to impose restrictions on off-road driving and at the same time restrict the number of vehicles and people allowed into the parks." In time, certain parks, like Amboseli and Lake Nakuru, will be developed for high density tourism, while others will remain low density, with more restrictions in terms of numbers of visitors.

Among Leakey's more controversial plans is the scheme to eventually fence most of Kenya's parks and reserves. The purpose is twofold: to aid in antipoaching efforts and to keep game from wandering onto private farmlands. The plan has drawn fire from conservationists who fear that such fencing would restrict migrations, having long-term impact on ecosystems by preventing animals from moving to new habitat. In particular, elephants need to range freely when, in the process of converting their woodland habitat to grassland, they find it necessary to move on to new areas. Leakey suggests, in such cases, that game migration corridors be established to allow such movement. In any event, he feels it important to minimize the adverse impact of game on agricultural lands. Otherwise, the continued conflict between people and game will be a losing one for wildlife.

Such plans may be a long time in the future, and Leakey has backed off from that early plan. The fencing scheme alone will be enormously expensive. In the short term, it has been necessary for Leakey to concentrate on solving Kenya's poaching problem, and thus far he has had great impact. When I spoke to him in February of 1990 he had been in office for slightly less than a year. "I'm still learning how to be a general," he admitted.

In Tanzania things have changed as well. Though statistics on poaching have not been as forthcoming as they have in Kenya, wildlife experts from African Wildlife Foundation agree that the combination of depressed ivory prices and stepped-up enforcement have drastically reduced elephant poaching. Tanzania's Director of Wildlife is Costa Mlay. While Mlay has received far less publicity and less funding than Richard Leakey, the consensus among wildlife researchers is that he has managed to get solid support and commitment from the Tanzanian government to carry out effective antipoaching work. Mlay credits the CITES ban in helping to stop the poaching. "There are more elephants to be seen all around, which is testimony to the validity and wisdom of the international community to ban the ivory trade." In a letter to the vice president of the International Wildlife Coalition, Mlay expresses concern about the future. "On our part, we do not think that what was achieved at Lausanne [the CITES meeting] is adequate or permanent. On the contrary, we must guard against the possibility of a resurgence of devastation such as was faced by the African elephant during the last ten years."

Citizen-funded conservation organizations continue to play a key role in aiding countries like Kenya and Tanzania. In 1990, the International Wildlife Coalition made a grant of $15,000 as a scholarship fund in Tanzania, established to provide education funds for the children of wildlife division rangers. A modest amount of money on the surface, it is of tremendous importance for these rangers whose annual salaries are so small. The award, according to Costa Mlay, was gratefully received.

As recipient of a $2.5 million grant from the U.S. Agency for International Development (AID), the African Wildlife Foundation will administer a program in Tanzania for protection of wildlife and utilization of such wildlife resources in the form of tourism. Again, a realistic goal for obtaining support for protection of Africa's game will come from people on a local level if it can be shown that they

Abdi Omar Bashir, deputy director of enforcement for the Kenya Wildlife Service, leads the war against poachers. "We've got good men now and we can win this war. We will win it. I promise you that this will be done."

Richard Leakey, director of the Kenya Wildlife Service. "We have an obligation here in Kenya to maintain our biodiversity."

can benefit economically. "We are even more proud of our several projects funded by many small donors, which concentrate on helping rural communities, Masai, and others to deal with their proximity to the elephants and national parks. It is called 'Neighbors as Partners' and operates in Uganda, Tanzania, and Kenya," said Diana McMeekin of the African Wildlife Foundation. The foundation has also played a key role in making the world aware of the elephant's plight and supports elephant research with funding for the projects of Joyce Poole and Cynthia Moss and others.

There are many unsung heroes in the war to save elephants. One of these is a remarkable lady I had the good fortune to meet in Nairobi. Her name is Daphne Sheldrick, widow of former Tsavo chief warden and noted Kenya conservationist David Sheldrick.

At her Animal Orphanage in the outskirts of Nairobi, adjacent to Nairobi National Park, Daphne has saved numerous infant elephants from death by starvation. The killing of adult elephants

for ivory is a tragedy, but equally tragic is the fate of youngsters orphaned by this carnage. Like human infants, young elephants cannot survive on their own. Without mothers and other family members to assist, youngsters die.

It hasn't been easy. "Elephants are by far the most difficult, most delicate, and most demanding of all animals to raise," she says. "In fact, it had once been considered impossible to hand-rear infant African elephants, for they are totally milk dependent for the first eighteen months of life and they cannot assimilate the fat of ordinary cow's milk." It took Daphne almost twenty-five years of experimentation to achieve the right combination of milk, food, and care in order to successfully raise the young elephants. One major breakthough was the development of a special milk formula from Wyeth Laboratories for human babies sensitive to regular milk. Because the formula is supplemented with vitamins and minerals, the baby elephants receive the nourishment vital to their growth and survival.

However, food alone doesn't ensure that her

One of the young elephants orphaned by poachers receives a special milk formula that saved it from starvation. Daphne Sheldrick's Animal Orphanage in Nairobi.

An old female with her weeks-old youngster alongside roams leisurely across grasslands in Amboseli National Park with ubiquitous cattle egrets following.

young animals will survive. In addition to ranking close to humans and apes in intelligence, elephants have a similar kind of development and life span to people. They reach puberty at twelve to fourteen years, are young adults at twenty, in their prime in their thirties and forties, and, with luck, live to age seventy or eighty. Social and maternal bonding is very strong among elephants—so much so that the death of mothers and relatives causes severe trauma in youngsters. According to Daphne, some infants have awakened screaming from nightmares the first few weeks at the ophanage. The orphanage attendants must spend twenty-four hours a day with their young charges, even sleeping with them in the stables at night, so strong are the youngsters' needs for loving companionship.

According to Daphne, "An elephant will thrive only if it is happy, and in order to be happy it must *never* be left alone again. Elephants also require mental stimulation—playthings and varied surroundings to combat boredom. But above all, they require a great deal of genuine and sincere *loving*."

The need for playthings I can certainly attest to. When I visited Daphne I met some of her young charges, among them a one-and-a-half year old male named Dika. The youngster had witnessed the slaughter of his mother and the entire herd by poachers. "On arrival he was so grief-stricken that he did not want to live for four months and was plagued with nightmares," said Daphne. Dika now seems on the road to recovery. I played a game of soccer with the young elephant, kicking the ball to him and then having him kick it back to me. He ran about like a little kid, ears flapping with joy. When he tired of the game, he took a mud bath and rolled about in the dirt, like any human youngster, with a look of ecstacy on his face.

Several of Daphne Sheldrick's elephants have been successfully reintroduced to the wild in Tsavo National Park. Sheldrick, like so many others, hopes that the worldwide ban on the sale and import of ivory will ensure their survival and prevent more elephants from being orphaned.

* * *

We have seen the last days of Eden. It would be nice to think that much of Africa can remain as wild and unfettered as it was fifty or a hundred years ago. A romantic notion, but unrealistic. Unfortunately. It's as unrealistic as keeping our own American West as wild as it was in the 1800s when the grizzly bear and the bison ruled the land. However, what can be realized in Africa is the continued preservation of reasonably sized blocks of land where whole ecosystems may remain relatively untouched. The rest of the civilized world needs to recognize an obligation to help such countries as Kenya, Tanzania, and others in implementing the protection of game from poaching, both by direct aid in support of antipoaching activities and continuing the ban on ivory products.

Will there be elephants and other African game in the twenty-first century? (In light of the way things are going, one might well ask if there'll be human beings in the twenty-first century.) The answer seems to be a tentative "Yes." Diana McMeekin is cautiously optimistic. "If we can keep the [CITES] ban in place for a while longer, the outlook is good." For how long? "Two decades, a generation of elephants, would give us a chance to observe how well they are recovering and whether there are long-term genetic or social problems. However, I'll settle for the year 2000 right now."

It is of great importance for the United States government to list the African elephant as an endangered species for all countries. That will prohibit, by law, any elephant products from being commercially imported into this country. At the moment it is *not* listed as endangered in Zimbabwe, South Africa, and Botswana. And as long as ivory from those countries can be imported, illegal, poached ivory will also be marketed, which means the continued slaughter of elephants everywhere.

When I spoke with Joyce Poole, she, too, expressed guarded hope. "As long as the ivory ban remains in place, I'm optimistic. But we need to be cautious because even though elephants may be increasing in numbers in some places, it doesn't mean that elephants are safe." What can each of us do to help elephants, aside from the obvious—refraining from buying ivory? "Learn more about elephants. And adopt an attitude that says 'elephants add something to my life.'"

* * *

From my notebook, dated March 12, 1991:

I write these notes in the company of elephants, in the fading light of my last day in Masai Mara. Tomorrow I fly back to Nairobi, then later tomorrow evening I board a jet for Zurich and New York. I don't like to think about that part of it. For now I savor these last few hours listening to

Dika, one of Daphne Sheldrick's orphaned elephants, plays a game of soccer with me. He's actually much better at it than I am.

Daphne Sheldrick and one of her youngsters orphaned by poaching. The elephants love their daily mud baths.

the melodic song of laughing doves, while watching these extraordinary animals as they graze placidly and speak to each other in cryptic rumblings.

Question: How important is it to keep in touch with other species that have shared the earth with us for a long time? Answer: Very. I think it's a mistake for us to assume that we can get along without them. Sharing the company of elephants, for example, is an experience that adds something important to my life. Without them I'm impoverished, intellectually and aesthetically. It's a chance to ponder, however briefly, our own origins on earth and to marvel at the infinitely rich variations of other species. Undoubtedly most of them can get along very well without us. That's a humbling thought and a blow to our technological egos, but it's true.

What will it all mean when I return to crowded freeways, frantic airline schedules, snarling taxi drivers, ringing telephones, editorial deadlines? Sanity. Peace. Solitude. And, at least for a while, realization that what I thought were major crises in my life aren't. Being here has been a chance to recalibrate and refresh some cluttered and overloaded brain cells.

It also means, at this very moment, a sense of joy and a sense of awe and wonder — the kind that we used to have as children, but as adults seem to have suppressed.

My friend Dave Brower, one of America's most articulate conservationists, sums it most succinctly: "Wipe out wilderness," he says, "and the world's a cage." He's right.

Kwaheri, ndovu. I'll see you next year. I hope.

There is nothing, absolutely nothing more frightening than an angry elephant. Whey they flare those ears and hold their heads high, you'd better back off — or else. This can be six tons of deadly fury.

ON SAFARI –
VISITING EAST AFRICA

After spending the night in a large, open grassy area, a family heads for a favorite feeding spot in a nearby forest. Masai Mara National Reserve, Kenya. (Photo © by Edward Borg.)

There are two basic ways of making an East African safari: 1) handling your own arrangements or 2) signing up with an established safari outfitter. I recommend the second, especially if this is your first trip. Making your own arrangements is not easy, and you could find yourself with a less-than-reliable vehicle or driver or both. Furthermore, a good guide-driver can make the trip so much more pleasurable. Unless you know the habits and the habitat of wildlife, you could miss a lot if you're on your own. I'm always amazed at the game-spotting skills of experienced guides.

For my own photo safaris, I use Voyagers International. President Dave Blanton has lived in Kenya for a number of years and knows the region well. Moreover, Voyagers brings meaning to the term *eco-tourism*. Everyone, from Dave to his assistants, exercises great care and sensitivity. This applies to the wildlife and to the people who sign up with them. I would be hard

pressed to find a better outfitter, and they are a great bargain to boot.

In Nairobi, East African Ornithological Safaris (EAOS) is, in my opinion, the best. They are used by Voyagers International, and the driver-guides (including my friend Lidede) are tops—good spotters and very knowledgeable about birds and game. The Turners, Don and Margaret and son Stephen, owners and founders of EAOS, are concerned and dedicated conservationists. In addition, if you sign up for a safari with EAOS or Voyagers, you get to stay at the Mara River Camp in Masai Mara—the only place to stay in that area. It is a small, comfortable tented lodge on the edge of the Mara River in the heart of the best game viewing in the region. Absolutely superb. If you make your own arrangements, at least reserve a place at Mara River Camp through EAOS or Voyagers.

People on their first safari often try to cram too much

into the trip. Here's a comfortable schedule for an eighteen-day safari in Kenya, including two days' air transport time on either end of the trip: overnight in Nairobi after arrival; two nights in either the Aberdares (the Ark) or Mt. Kenya (Mountain Lodge); four nights in Samburu/Buffalo Springs National Reserve; two nights at either Lake Baringo or Lake Nakuru; and five nights in Masai Mara. This allows sufficient time to experience — and photograph — a variety of superb ecosystems with different wildlife. For longer safaris, you could add Tsavo and perhaps Amboseli national parks. In Tanzania, a good eighteen-day itinerary includes two nights in Tarangire National Park, a night or two at Lake Manyara, and the rest of the time divided between Ngorongoro Crater and Serengeti National Park. Voyagers can work out a combination trip, with part of the time spent in Tanzania and part in Kenya.

Choosing the time of year for your safari is important. January, February, and March in both Kenya and Tanzania are excellent times. January is calving time for wildebeest in Serengeti and Masai Mara. July and August are the months of the incredible wildebeest migration from Serengeti to Masai Mara, which means that there's little game in Serengeti at that time. Ngorongoro, however, is still good.

A few tips on photo gear and film before you leave for your trip: Good wildlife photography on safari requires long telephotos, even though, on occasion, your driver can closely approach certain animals. A good choice for long lens is a 400mm, together with a 1.4 extender, making it a 560mm lens. For other lenses, I suggest everything from 20mm or 24mm ultra-wide-angles to zoom lenses ranging from 35-70mm and 70-210mm. Choose different film speeds — slow to medium speed (ISO 50 or 64) for fine grain, to higher speed film such as Kodachrome 200 when using long lenses in low light. And bring some 100 — Fujichrome 100 or Ektachrome 100. Quantity? If you're a serious photographer and want to come back with the best shots, be prepared to shoot lots. I suggest you allow for ten rolls per shooting day in the parks and reserves (this doesn't include days of driving between parks).

Voyagers International
P.O. Box 915
Ithaca, New York 14851
Phone: 607-257-3091
FAX: 607-257-3699

East African Ornithological Safaris
P.O. Box 48019
Nairobi, Kenya
Phone: 331684
FAX: 216528

If you're interested in photo safaris, arranged through Voyagers and East African Ornithological:

Wilderness Photography Workshops
P.O. Box 2605
Evergreen, Colorado 80439
Phone: 303-674-3009
FAX: 303-674-7022

In the shade of a tree in Kenya's Samburu National Reserve, this female strikes an unusual pose.

HOW YOU CAN HELP THE AFRICAN ELEPHANT

Continued research and constant vigilance are still required to assure the survival of the African elephant. Contact these organizations to find out how you can help them carry out these tasks.

African Wildlife Foundation
1717 Massachusetts Avenue Northwest
Washington, D.C. 20036

Elefriends
Cherry Tree Cottage
Coldharbour
Dorking, Surrey RH5 6HA

Global Communications for Conservation
(Funds for the Kenya Wildlife Service can be specified for elephant research and conservation)
150 East 58th Street
New York, NY 10155
(Also look for an upcoming office in the United Kingdom.)

International Wildlife Coalition
P.O. Box 138
Elisberry, MO 63343

Kenya Wildlife Fund—Canada
P.O. Box 2445, Station B
Richmond Hill, Ontario L4E 1A5

World Wildlife Fund—Canada
60 St. Clair Avenue East
Suite 201
Toronto, Ontario M4T 1N5

World Wildlife Fund—United States
1250 24th Street Northwest
Washington, D.C. 20037

World Wildlife Fund—United Kingdom
Panda House
Weyside Park
Godalming, Surrey GU7 1XR

NOTES ON
THE PHOTOGRAPHY

Dawn in Masai Mara National Reserve. Three big males wander leisurely, feeding on grasses as the sun comes up.

For an animal so big, elephants can sometimes be elusive. I've spent many hours waiting for a family group or lone individuals to move out of forest cover into open areas where the photography is a bit better. Sometimes, returning to the same place where I had left a family of elephants on the previous evening, I discovered that they had disappeared—from the whole area! So, for anyone interested in pursuing elephant photography in a serious way, I have two words of advice: patience and persistence.

Patience is especially important in capturing some of the marvelous behavior of these animals, such as touching or sparring or play among the youngsters (and sometimes the oldsters). I've often sat for hours in my vehicle watching and photographing a family group. Other vehicles come by, the occupants stop for a picture or two, and then they roar off in a cloud of dust. It's too bad, because these people miss a lot.

The pictures in this book were made with Leica R4, R5, and R6 cameras and Leica lenses, with occasional use of some older, nonelectronic Nikons. As more and more of my work takes me to more and more remote parts of the world, I've grown very distrustful of these fancy autofocus, fully electronic cameras. They don't seem to hold up well in cold climates, soggy rain forests, or the heat and dust of Africa. Maybe someday they'll be reliable, but in the meantime, I can't take a chance on the failure of delicate electronics.

All pictures were made with manual-focus lenses. I know, it sounds like heresy in this era of autofocus, but the times I've tried autofocus lenses, *they've actually slowed me down.* With my manual focus lenses, I can focus *and* compose the picture simultaneously. With autofocus, it's necessary to center the subject, let the lens focus, then lock the focus, recompose the picture, then shoot. As I said, too slow. With animals so large, it might seem that long telephotos are unnecessary. Actually, by using 400mm or 560mm lenses, I can stay well back from families or individuals and not influence their behavior. This is especially important when family members are engaged in play or greeting each other or expressing affection. When vehicles approach too closely, the elephants tend to get a little nervous and stop whatever they're engaged in.

My film choices depend on conditions. Early morning or late afternoon light dictates use of Kodachrome 200. Midmorning and midafternoon shots will allow use of slower films such as Kodachrome 64, Fujichrome Velvia (ISO 50), or Ektachrome 100 Plus Professional. Fujichrome Velvia has especially rich, saturated colors. Regardless of film choice, I try to avoid shooting during midday when the light is very harsh and high in contrast.

REFERENCES

Three elephants greet each other at a water hole near a river. The touching of trunks is a common greeting and a means of expressing affection. (Photo © by Edward Borg.)

Amin, Mohamed. *Kenya,* Nairobi, Kenya: Spectrum Guide to Kenya, 1989.

Beard, Peter H. *End of the Game: The Last Word From Paradise,* San Francisco, CA: Chronicle Books, 1988.

Cole, Sonia. *The Prehistory of East Africa,* Middlesex, England: Penguin Books, 1954.

Dinesen, Isak. *Out of Africa,* Middlesex, England: Penguin Books, 1985.

Dorst, Jean, and Dandelot, Pierre. *A Field Guide to the Larger Mammals of Africa,* London: Collins, 1984.

Douglas-Hamilton, Iain and Oria. *Among the Elephants,* New York: Viking Press, 1975.

Hemingway, Ernest. *The Green Hills of Africa,* New York: Macmillan, 1987.

Holman, Dennis. *Massacre of the Elephants,* New York: Holt, Rinehart, and Winston, 1967.

Leakey, Richard E., and Lewin, Roger. *Origins,* New York: E. P. Dutton, 1982.

Luard, Nicholas. *The Wildlife Parks of Africa,* Salem, NH: Salem House, 1986.

Markham, Beryl. *West With the Night,* Berkeley, CA: North Point Press, 1983.

Matthiessen, Peter. *The Tree Where Man Was Born,* New York: Crescent Books, 1975.

Moss, Cynthia. *Elephant Memories,* New York: William Morrow and Co., 1988.

Parker, Ian, and Amin, Mohamed. *Ivory Crisis,* Nairobi, Kenya: Camerapix, 1983.

Patterson, J. H. *The Man-Eaters of Tsavo,* New York: St. Martin's Press, 1986.

Savage, R. J. G. *Mammal Evolution: An Illustrated Guide,* New York, Facts on File, 1986.

Turner, Myles. *My Serengeti Years,* New York: W. W. Norton, 1988.

Williams, Heathcote. *Sacred Elephant,* New York: Harmony Books, 1989.

Williams, J. G. *Field Guide to the National Parks of East Africa,* London: Collins, 1984.

Overleaf: A lone elephant wanders in Masai Mara National Reserve in Kenya.